The
Economist

MARKETING FOR GROWTH

The role of marketers in driving revenues
and profits

Iain Ellwood

D0280803

THE ECONOMIST IN ASSOCIATION WITH
PROFILE BOOKS LTD

Published by Profile Books Ltd
3a Exmouth House
Pine Street
London EC1R OJH
www.profilebooks.com

Typeset in EcoType by MacGuru Ltd
info@macguru.org.uk

Printed in Great Britain by Clays, Bungay, Suffolk

A CIP catalogue record for this book is available from the British Library

Hardback ISBN: 978 1 84668 904 8
Paperback ISBN: 978 1 84668 905 5
e-book ISBN: 978 1 84765 865 4

FSC
www.fsc.org
MIX
Paper from
responsible sources
FSC® C018072

The paper this book is printed on is certified by the
© 1996 Forest Stewardship Council A.C. (FSC).
It is ancient-forest friendly. The printer holds FSC chain of custody SGS-COC-2061

To Hannah

Contents

Acknowledgements   viii
Introduction   ix

1 Customer value management   1
2 Return on investment: measurement and analytics   16
3 Barriers to growth   40
4 Targeting customers and external stakeholders   51
5 Market opportunities for growth   67
6 Proposition definition   90
7 Brand portfolio growth   106
8 Growth through employee engagement   132
9 Growth through customer engagement   150
10 Growing service-based brands   175

Glossary   185
Sources   190
Further reading   195
Index   197

Acknowledgements

MANY PEOPLE HAVE HELPED make this book possible.

First, I would like to thank those who have helped shape my thinking and been a source of much support and advice over the years: my parents, Jan and Robert Ellwood, my brothers, Andrew and Peter, Raymond Blanc, Simona Botti, Charlie Colquhoun, Paul Crisford, Simon Crisford, Morag Cuddeford-Jones, Jack Fraser, Adrian Furnham, Alastair Kingsland, David Martin, Noel Penrose, Evgeniya Petrova, Alistair Robinson, Kirsty Ross, Teresa Schrezenmaier and Grant Usmar.

I have worked with many business leaders to whom I am grateful for their expertise and experiences, including John Allert, Fred Brown, Rita Clifton, Isabelle M. Conner, Julian Dailly, Gabor Dani, Adi Godrej, Dominic Grounsell, Tiffany Hall, Chris Kersebergen, Larry Light, Andy Milligan, Geraldine O'Connell, Clare Salmon, Simon Scoot, Simon Smith and David Still. I also owe a special debt to Frances Frei, UPS Foundation Professor of Service Management at Harvard Business School, whose teaching inspired me to champion brand marketing as a more effective way to generate profitable business growth.

On the publishing side, Stephen Brough and Penny Williams made all the difference with their clear and patient guidance. Thanks to them and everyone at Profile Books.

Most of all I would like to thank my wife, Hannah, to whom this book is dedicated, and without whose support and love I could not have written a word.

Iain Ellwood
November 2013

Introduction

MARKETING IS THE STRUCTURED PROCESS of targeting and engaging new and current customers in order to generate sales. Marketers, therefore, play a crucial role in generating revenue and they can play an equally important role in how revenues translate into profit. This is a guide to how marketers can improve their commercial focus and become more influential drivers of business growth. Businesses grow by becoming better at what they do, and by being smarter or more efficient, and this involves developing and improving products, processes, people and standards of service. Part of the marketing role is to pick up on changing customer needs and behaviour and the forces at play in markets – and to do so ahead of the competition. If marketers do this well, they will increase their business's prospects for growth, and their influence and impact within the business.

This book focuses on the role of marketers – and the tools and methods available to them – in identifying and achieving profitable growth. It puts marketing and marketers at the commercial heart of a business with responsibility for strengthening the links between a business's operations and its customers. It examines each part of the growth life cycle, starting with the use of analytics to define the financial size of the prize and to measure the impact of marketing. It explains how to identify the more potentially rewarding customer targets, define more relevant and differentiated customer propositions, and make sure that employees deliver what is promised and that customers become greater advocates for the brand. It reinforces the need for marketing activities to be directly underpinned by strong commercial financial outcomes.

For marketers tired of being viewed by some as a "cost", the challenge is to take more responsibility for the commercial results of the company. By becoming more financially fluent as well as more accountable and responsible for the commercial outcomes, they will gain greater authority and influence. This may require the development of new skills as well as an attitudinal shift, whereby they see themselves and behave as asset managers making investment and return decisions.

About this book

Each chapter is designed to stand on its own, and together the ten chapters are intended to form a convenient handbook of insights, methods, frameworks and tools for marketers to help them drive growth in their organisations. The chapters deal with the following:

1 **Customer value management** describes the importance of linking marketing activities with commercial outcomes and outlines the main ways that marketing can increase revenues and profits.

2 **Return on investment: measurement and analytics** defines the many different ways to statistically quantify the effectiveness of marketing activities and help predict future returns. The huge amount of customer data that is now available means marketers can make fact-based decisions about new business growth opportunities; prioritise which will deliver the best financial returns and decide how to best spend their marketing budgets.

3 **Barriers to growth** describes the biases that reduce the effectiveness of decision-making by business leaders, providing simple techniques that can help overcome these human traits that might limit growth.

4 **Targeting customers and external stakeholders** defines the different ways of identifying the most valuable customers. Analysis of demographic and attitudinal characteristics helps make sure that new products and services deliver what customers want or need. Targeting a specific segment or part of the population helps companies to manage their resources and gain the best return on investment.

5 Market opportunities for growth defines ways to analyse business growth opportunities and prioritise investment in them. In order to arrive at an appropriate balance of risk and reward, this should take account of the needs of current and future customers, and the nature of current and future markets.

6 Proposition definition describes how to create a brand proposition that will be compelling to new and current customers. It looks at the importance of a proposition's practical and emotional relevance to customers, its differentiation from the competition and its authenticity, and how the proposition must be reflected in the actual customer experience.

7 Brand portfolio growth describes how an organisation's brands can be managed to maximise its overall growth. This might be through a single master brand or a range of different brands for different customer segments.

8 Growth through employee engagement outlines the positive difference a high level of employee commitment and engagement makes to the performance of a business. It explores the importance of clear vision, shared values and common behaviour, and describes how to create and manage an effective employee engagement programme.

9 Growth through customer engagement defines the most effective ways to engage and influence potential and current customers. It describes how digital and mobile media are having a dramatic effect on how companies connect with their customers and it outlines a framework for improving customer engagement.

10 Growing service-based brands looks at the particular difficulties faced by service businesses and how marketing can help overcome them. It highlights the importance of process design, pricing strategy and frontline employees in dealing with the various issues.

There is also a glossary of terms and concepts used in marketing.

1 Customer value management

A 2012 SURVEY among chief marketing officers (CMOs) commissioned by Senate, a consulting firm, identified that marketing ranked fourth out of seven board functions behind corporate strategy, sales and product development, and only just ahead of the finance, IT and human resources teams at bringing growth opportunities to the board. The same survey revealed that only 23% of corporate boards are given data relating to customer lifetime value (CLV) that among other things identifies their most and least profitable customers.

Customer value management is crucial to achieving the primary goal of marketing: that is, to increase the number of customers and increase profit per customer. Yet the marketing department will only establish its credentials at board level as an important driver of a company's profits by demonstrating that it is commercially "literate" – that it fully grasps the business's commercial and accounting processes and principles. It must also manage, analyse and communicate its activities and output in financial terms that directors understand and appreciate. In short, marketers need to link their strategy and activities directly with revenue and profit growth.

Customer value management depends on defining marketing activities that make the most impact on the way that business is run and relating them to commonly used commercial and accounting measures, notably shareholder value, revenue and profit growth and customer lifetime value.

Shareholder value creation

An aim – the overriding aim according to many – of a company is to create value for its owners, what is commonly referred to as shareholder value. Chief executives typically focus on measures such as the share price and dividend. Others, such as investors, analysts and predators, may be just as if not more interested in the free cash flow that the business generates beyond its operational costs. It is the ability to generate cash that makes a business attractive – because cash is real whereas profit is an accounting concept. The free cash flow a business is able to generate involves four factors:

- **Level of cash flow.** How much can cash flow be increased? The greater the cash flow, the more valuable the business.

- **Speed of cash flow.** How quickly can cash be generated? Getting $1,000 today is worth more than $1,000 tomorrow because today's money can be put to work earning yet more money sooner than tomorrow's. The quicker the cash comes in, the greater the value to the business.

- **Sustainability of revenues.** How long lasting is this revenue? The more a business is able to maintain its advantage over competitors and sustain its revenues and profits, the more valuable it will be.

- **Risks affecting future cash flow.** How secure is future revenue? Customers, markets and businesses change, and so the more protected and less volatile the cash flow, the greater the value of the business.

Applying a marketing perspective

The way that marketers can have an impact on these four cash flow factors is as follows:

- Level of cash flow – increase sales revenue through enhanced attractiveness and relevance to the customer and through differentiation of the company's offering in its market segment.

- Speed of cash flow – gain and serve customers quicker and better through smarter segmentation, targeting and customer engagement.

- Sustainability of revenues – build strong brands.
- Risks affecting future cash flow – build loyalty with customers and increase the overall strength of the business's portfolio of products and services. Branding again plays an important role here.

Revenue and profit growth

Growth is accelerated through increasing revenues and extending profit margins.

A 2011 *McKinsey Quarterly* study, "Drawing a new road map for growth", highlighted that most businesses achieve more of their revenue growth from developing the market than from winning market share. This means managing growth at a product or customer-segment level rather than at a macro level such as the overall brand or product portfolio. Revenue growth comes from specific customers, not customers in general. Marketers, with their proximity to customers and markets, are ideally placed to identify shifts in customer trends and buying patterns, and as a result identify opportunities for market development. The data that marketing departments routinely gather and the insight that data provides helps them identify new prospects and refine the offering. It is never enough in the longer term simply to

FIG 1.1 **Revenue and profit growth options**

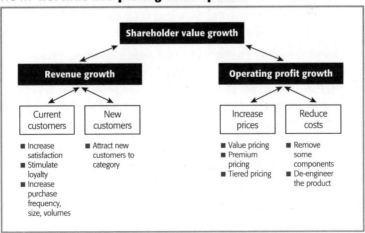

play catch-up with your competitors, and it is extremely dangerous to edge into complacency once you have overtaken them. With an eye to growth, marketers must constantly use their experience to sharpen specific propositions around new growth areas.

Customer value management

As the marketing department has responsibility for the relationship with the customer it should take its share of rightful responsibility for customer profitability. This requires marketers to get to grips with what exactly profit is and how it is created, and how products and sales and service offers need to be adapted to increase profitability. Customer value management helps businesses to identify their most profitable customers and tune their offers to increase profitability. This includes developing an understanding not only of today's most profitable customers but also of those who might be profitable in the future. Working out sales and profit per customer minus the cost to acquire and serve that customer helps here as it gives the marketer a view of the overall customer lifetime value associated with a product. Calculating the CLV gives the longer-term value of each customer. Short-term figures are unreliable indicators as they may reflect spikes resulting from, say, discounting.

The CLV brings together estimates of three elements:

- The typical lifetime of a customer. For a car or detergent brand, this might be 40–50 years; for a magazine aimed at teenagers, it might be only three years.
- The year-by-year revenues of a customer, based on product price and the frequency/volume of purchases. Car revenues per customer might be $30,000 every five years (annual value $6,000, total value $240,000–300,000) while the magazine might be $4 per month (annual value $48, total value $144).
- The one-off cost to acquire the customer and the cost to serve or deliver the product. For the car, this should include all elements of acquisition such as advertising and car dealership costs, the product costs and any annual servicing included in the offer to purchasers. For the magazine, it might include celebrity

sponsorship, production costs as well as distribution and website costs.

From these three estimates it is now possible to calculate the net present value (NPV) of the future revenue stream from a customer or customer segment. The NPV is the value now of a future stream of cash flows, adjusted by a discount rate. The discount rate takes into account the fact that $100 today is more valuable than $100 in the future. The rate used is meant to reflect the risk that the future cash flow will not materialise and the cost of borrowing should it not. In simple terms, if the estimated discount rate is 10%, for a future cash flow of $1,000 the NPV is $909. In other words, the future value of $1,000 is discounted by $91. With a time value of money of 10%, $909 can be invested today and will grow by $91 ($909 × 10%) to be $1,000 in one year.

This type of analysis will help establish which customer segments make the most money for the business. It will also help draw attention to those which are not sufficiently profitable because, for example, they are too costly in terms of time and money to attract or to serve.

Most businesses have a rump of customers who are not profitable but who, perhaps because they are loyal, provide a useful revenue stream with low ongoing investment costs. This is covered in detail in Chapter 4.

Figure 1.2 illustrates how the profitability of different customer segments can vary – in this case from the most profitable segments where each customer has a lifetime value of between $60,000 and $80,000 to those segments where customers are unprofitable and can be said to be destroying value, and who therefore should be discouraged or avoided, unless there is a way their profitability can be improved. Analysis should focus on the steepness of the profitability line; a steep difference between the highly profitable customers and those that break even indicates that most of the profits come from a hard core of customers. Many loyalty schemes recognise and acknowledge this by "ranking" and rewarding customers according to their value; for example, InterContinental Hotels Group uses the Ambassador level of its Priority Rewards Club to provide additional benefits for its most valuable customers. (Loyalty programmes

FIG 1.2 **Customer segment profitability differences**
$

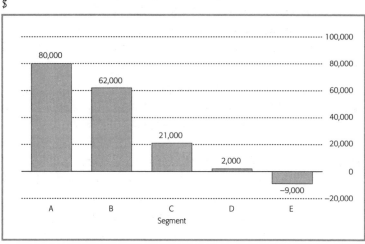

are covered in more detail in Chapter 10.) For customers that are unprofitable, it is important to discover whether their profitability can be improved before you give up on them. For example, high-data-use mobile phone users used to be highly unprofitable, but now they are the most profitable customer segment as they are the most frequent users of associated paid-for mobile services such as apps.

Grow customer revenues

Sophisticated NPV analysis requires intelligent and efficient data management without which it is hard for managers to make the best investment decisions. Taking it step by step, starting with a simple segment-based lifetime customer value, will help a business get to the desired level of sophistication. As well as NPV analysis there are a number of other measures that can help determine where greater customer value can be unlocked. For example:

- **Purchase frequency.** Can customers be tempted to buy a product or service more frequently?
- **Basket size.** Also known as cross-selling or upselling. Can customers be encouraged to buy an additional product (cross-selling) or a bigger/more expensive product (upselling)?

- **Share of wallet.** Can a specific store, product or brand become the customer's preferred store, product or brand?
- **Marketing costs.** Can marketing spend be reduced or redirected because customers are acting as advocates for the product, brand or store.

Improvements in any of these aspects will be good for a business, but knowing which make the biggest difference makes it clear where to focus. There are a number of things that marketers can do.

Increase the number of profitable customers

The aim should be to increase the number of the most valuable customers, while not putting off others who are profitable. The development of a strong and clear brand identity helps attract the customers you want while deterring those you do not want. Creating a halo effect also helps – customers who because of their experience of one branded product feel favourable towards other similarly branded products. The halo effect works in other ways too. Travel firms seek out the adventurous segment because it is a small but profitable group of travellers who purchase frequently at high prices and are easy to serve. For a travel brand, its appeal to that segment can also act as a draw to the many other travellers who have aspirations to be more adventurous.

Increase cross-selling and upselling

Once a customer has chosen your product, you can find out more about them and their needs and introduce them to or develop other products that they might like. A range of product variations can be developed that encourage customers to gradually move up the range as they become more sophisticated in their choice or their needs change. Or completely new product ranges can be introduced as firms get a deeper knowledge of their customers' needs and purchasing behaviour.

Supermarkets have been adept at expanding into non-food sales. In the United States, Target sells a wide range of grocery and non-food products, as well as own-label brands such as Up and Up, Archer

Farm and Market Pantry. Tesco's Florence & Fred clothing range now accounts for some £1 billion of the British retailer's revenues or 15% of total turnover and has a higher profit margin than its grocery business. Moreover, as banks lose their lustre, the big retail groups have been quick to move into financial services; Tesco's banking service accounts for just 1.3% of total turnover and 7% of total profits.

Increase price by delivering higher value

Virgin Atlantic's Upper Class service from major cities provides not just a luxury seat on a plane but also a series of additional benefits. These include high-speed motorbike or car transport to the airport, a VIP lounge with a spa, restaurant and bar, as well as an in-flight bar and a massage. All these additional experiences help strengthen the brand's value and appeal to customers. When the journey time is the same whatever class of seat you have paid for, it is such differences that make all the difference.

In a world in which products and services have to a large extent become standardised commodities, it is the additional benefits that create the most differentiation and which enable a premium price to be charged. In their book *The Experience Economy*, B. Joseph Pine and James Gilmore explore the concept that people will pay more for rich, engaging "experiences" than for simple products or services, and that the more emotionally appealing the experience, the higher the price people are willing to pay. Dining at The Ivy in Beverley Hills carries a huge emotional significance that far outweighs its simple interior or the fact that you are paying $40 for a lettuce that you can buy in a store for $1.50. Diners are paying for exclusivity, top-quality food, drama and celebrity sheen, resulting in an unforgettable evening. The price they are willing to pay for this runs to hundreds of dollars a head, well beyond the "cost" of delivery.

Increase the durability of customer relationships

The stronger and longer the relationship, the better it is for future cash flows. Porsche, a premium car brand, found that there was often a finite length to its relationship with many of its (mostly) young male customers. Loyalty scores among Porsche owners were high until they reached their 30s and had families that the sports cars could not comfortably accommodate. Porsche's response was to introduce the four-door Cayenne sports utility vehicle (SUV). By creating an additional, family-friendly product Porsche was able to continue to satisfy customers' needs and extend the relationship. The resulting boost to profits through sales of the Cayenne was 22% in 2011.

Meeting a customer's original need is just the first necessary step in creating the emotional bond that will tie the customer to a brand for the longer term. Customers expect a better level of service with brands to which they have a longer-term commitment than they do when they make a one-off transaction. Such longer-term relationships are often cemented by the benefits provided in addition to the functional ones the brand provides, rewards programmes run by airlines, coffee shops, supermarkets and other retailers. There is reciprocity. Everyone wins: the customers get more for their money, and the costs to the company of providing such benefits are usually significantly lower than the costs of acquiring new customers; furthermore, it already knows that these customers are satisfied fans of the brand.

Reduce the cost of acquiring customers

Finding new customers and convincing them to try a new product or switch from their current supplier is a high-cost process. Getting the cost/benefit balance right is difficult, and there can be no doubt that too much time and money is often spent by marketers on getting people to try something new. However, there are some important differences in how to approach the process between high-growth developing markets and mature developed markets with little or no growth.

In emerging markets, where product ownership levels are low, there are plenty of people who have yet to try and buy new and existing products and services. So the traditional marketing approach of using television advertising to raise awareness of a product, combined with a discount voucher to encourage people to try a new product can work well. But in mature markets, the emphasis needs to be on increasing share of wallet from existing customers. This requires a different set of skills and careful thought, rather than razzmatazz

– which may explain why it does not always get the attention it should from marketing teams. Marketers should never lose sight of the fact that it is less expensive to delight customers who already buy a product than it is to attract and satisfy new ones. Loyal customers are usually more profitable because they cost less to serve. Too many marketing teams focus on the wrong things, spending too much time trying to push new products onto new or unwilling customers rather than nurturing the ones they already have. For businesses with low customer satisfaction, there is little sense in striving to attract new customers when they are no more likely to be satisfied than the existing unhappy customers, who themselves may well be deterring new ones through word of mouth. Throwing money at getting new customers will not deal with the root of the problem: that customers do not like what the company is selling. However, there is only so much that existing customers can buy, and there will be times when there is a strong business case for a campaign to attract new customers.

Generating awareness of a product or service and acquiring new customers is one of the costliest marketing activities. It becomes even more costly to the business if new customers spend little and develop no loyalty to the brand. For marketers, proliferation of the ways to get marketing messages across has not made their job easier. In recent years there has been a shift away from expensive broadcast TV advertising towards narrowcast, emotionally engaging channels such as sponsorship events, forums, blogs and social media. Sponsorship events are effective because company and customers meet face-to-face, often in an energising and dramatic context like motor racing or athletics competitions. Social media are equally engaging as they allow customers to express their opinions to each other and to the company. This instant feedback is critical to customers' initial choice of brand. Investing in social media and customer service is the best way to improve the quantity and quality of peer-group reviews.

The costs associated with acquiring new customers include the costs of telling people about the product as well as those associated with selling and delivering the product or service to them. A classic method of reducing customer acquisition costs is a "member gets member" programme. Citibank offered its American Citigold customers cash for introducing new customers for current accounts. Both the referrer and the referred customer benefited from the programme, with the referrer receiving $100 for each new customer (with a maximum of five customers or $500) and each newly referred customer received $100 for opening a Citigold relationship package.

Increase customer engagement

Getting customers engaged involves building their awareness of a product and demonstrating its relevance to them. This is covered in more detail in Chapter 9. The process may include activities such as advertising in all its forms, sponsorship, PR and promotions, as well as direct mailing through letters as well as online, events and product trials. The media buying costs (of advertising, especially expensive media like TV and print) are usually the most significant proportion of expenditure, although advertising-agency production charges can be high for high-quality materials. Firms with strong brands like BMW and American Express use their most loyal customers as advocates for their products. This might simply be using them in advertisements, showing them as happy customers. But they also use some customers to provide other customers and potential customers with advice and information about their products. These zealous advocates can be highly persuasive because, being unpaid volunteers, they are perceived to be objective about the brand.

Increase customer satisfaction

The costs of selling and delivering products or services to customers can be high and is covered in Chapter 9. To reduce their costs or improve their offering, many companies have outsourced some of the services they provide. Sprint, an American mobile brand, outsourced part of its network in a $5 billion deal with Ericsson. The benefits included improvement in the quality of its network coverage. But it has become clear that many of these business process outsourcing (BPO) arrangements have had the effect of leaving customers feeling underserved and less satisfied; furthermore, many are not delivering the level of reduced costs that was anticipated. With costs in China and India increasing by some 17–20% a year and customers being prepared to pay extra for local call centres, more and more companies are re-shoring activities that they had outsourced offshore.

The cost of selling has traditionally been the responsibility of the marketing function and the cost of delivery has been that of those running operations, but it has become more common for sales and marketing and delivery to be combined. By removing interdepartmental duplication, contradiction and turf wars, there is greater coherence and efficiency, and everything works much more seamlessly and satisfyingly for the customer.

Reduce the cost of serving customers

The aim with any profitable customers is to make sure that they become or remain regular purchasers of one or more of the company's products or services. Even with currently unprofitable customers, it is rare that after an analysis of their needs they cannot be transformed into profitable ones, and it is unwise to discard them too readily. Finding ways to reduce the cost of serving any and all customers can, as the opportunities offered by the internet have shown, turn unprofitable customers into profitable ones and provide a substantial boost to the bottom line.

Customer relationship management

Customer relationship management (CRM) systems are used to manage customers on a more individual basis and help identify sales opportunities. CRM systems rely on big data analysis of individual customer data to make adjustments to marketing activity. Big data is the common term for large-scale data banks of customer information gained from their shopping activities including credit-card, mobile phone and website usage. A global phone provider, for example, knows the amount of texts, phone calls and internet usage of every customer – where they were, how long they took and which websites they looked at. This kind of information gives a business a detailed picture of its customers' habits. Home Depot, an American DIY retail chain, has successfully used CRM to develop an e-newsletter with customised content to drive its high-value members to "The Garden Club" and "My Outdoor" sections of its website. Social media were used to encourage these members to share tips and style preferences with like-minded members.

CRM can also be used defensively to reduce the risk of customers going elsewhere. Ocado, an online retailer, tracks individual transactions to identify changes in customer behaviour. For example, a customer may have recently started buying baby food and therefore would benefit from a "family voucher" or shopping suggestions. The data can also be used to identify when customers are unlikely to make another purchase. In Ocado's case, this is when they have bought nothing for more than two weeks. They are then e-mailed a money-off voucher. For customers, the offer of a large saving usually encourages them to keep on using the service. Of course, savvy shoppers can work out these threshold tactics and hold off shopping until they get their voucher, but a good CRM system should be able to adapt to such behaviour.

CRM enables the targeting of promotions that increase basket size or loyalty. However, it can prove expensive to implement a coherent company-wide CRM system because of the way different departments have evolved and handle data capture and analysis. Equally, data capture through loyalty cards, online shopping and social media provides a wealth of data that it can be tempting to overanalyse and overuse, resulting in misconceived or uneconomic campaigns. Furthermore, a company with a lot of data at its fingertips may fall foul of data protection rules, or find that the costs of managing and monitoring its activities become an unwanted and distracting burden.

But CRM has become well entrenched in modern business and the drive to expand and secure the customer base. In the notoriously high-churn mobile telecommunications market, O2 has used CRM to introduce a number of services that enable it to make individual offers to its customers which avoid wastage and increase satisfaction. CRM enables companies to carry out:

- **Real-time sales analysis.** By knowing what is bought, by whom, where, how often and when, a business can match supply more accurately with demand and reduce wasted capacity or stock.
- **Customer profiling and behavioural analysis.** This is the precise segmentation of customers that enables changes in

buying behaviour to be identified – for example, when couples split up or have a child or move jobs and houses.

■ **Campaign effectiveness analysis.** It is only through knowing what customers did following a campaign that you can really know how effective the campaign was, and therefore how you can make future campaigns more cost effective.

■ **Loyalty analysis.** This enables a firm to track the behaviour of regular customers and to identify which purchasers are likely to become long-term regular customers – and when.

■ **Profitability analysis.** This enables the identification of customers who are becoming less profitable, as well as those whose are becoming more valuable and may be ripe for special treatment such as an upgrade in loyalty-card status.

The advantages of simplicity

The profitability of underperforming products or services can often be increased by simplifying the offering, as has happened with the emphasis many firms have put on their online presence as a means of encouraging customers to "self-serve". For example, low-cost insurance policies are now often sold online through a process that involves automated checklists, algorithms and databases to set prices. Alternatively, marketers may be able to modify their offering, perhaps by providing fewer features to less profitable customers or charging a premium for an enhanced service. Each customer segment's unmet needs and drivers of satisfaction need to be analysed in order to shape different offers that will deliver the intended outcome. For the bulk of customers, there should be ways to improve low profitability.

Sometimes it is the simpler product that gives a business a competitive advantage. Until recently, bicycles had to have many gears, often 15 or 20, for them to be considered high-end. But fixed-gear bikes with stripped-back features have become more popular, with those buying these "Fixie" bikes being happy to pay more for much less. The overall profitability of these bikes is much higher than the more complex products because they do a single thing really well without the cost of added complexity. Companies should be wary of getting into a features "arms race" with their competitors, as this will increase cost to serve and almost certainly reduce profitability because of competitive pressure on price.

Summary

Customer value management is at the heart of increasing a business's profitable growth, and because the marketing department is responsible for the relationship with the customer, it should take responsibility for helping to set and achieve revenue and profit targets. Marketers must therefore become comfortable with and well versed in using well-established financial concepts such as NPV. By defining what customers mean to an organisation in terms of their cost and profit to acquire and serve, marketers can demonstrate their tangible contribution to the financial performance of their business while establishing greater boardroom credibility. In a fast-changing world, such analysis will also help them adjust their strategy and plans to what will best generate profitable growth for the business – which may well not be what has worked in the past.

2 Return on investment: measurement and analytics

THE ROLE MARKETING PLAYS has a critical impact on the financial performance of a business, yet many still feel that marketing is a discipline that is hard to align to anything other than soft measures such as brand consideration (how many people might consider a particular brand) or brand equity (what attributes – such as friendliness or trust – are associated with a specific brand). In the 2011 IBM Global CMO Study nearly two-thirds of respondents (63%) rated return on investment (ROI) as the most important measure, but fewer than half (44%) felt capable of measuring it accurately.

Marketing has clearly moved on from the heady days of the 1950s and 1960s when the ability to engage a stellar advertising agency and post a billboard was enough to establish a brand's status. Greatly increased competition, global markets and a proliferation of media channels make it much more difficult to decide how to allocate marketing spend – and to justify what is spent on what. Even in healthy economic times, there is much less of an appetite than before for the big spend unless it is linked to clear business results. But it is possible to link information about customers' needs, preferences, habits and behaviour to the financial impact of a business's sales and marketing activities. It comes down to making sure that the right thing is being measured. There are four stages of information gathering and analysis that will help marketers develop a business case for a marketing strategy:

■ **Insight gathering.** Using proprietary and third-party information to assess marketing performance and investment choices.

- **Investment prioritisation analysis.** Determining where the business needs marketing support to deliver the greatest returns.
- **Linkage to commercial results.** Placing marketing activity in a financial context using insight gathering and investment prioritisation analysis in conjunction with other research and analysis such as data mining, which is discussed later in this chapter.
- **Strategic marketing analytics.** Using concepts explained below such as brand valuation, the purchase funnel and the net promoter score (NPS) to make decisions more focused on the strategic direction of the organisation as a whole rather than one part of it.

Insight gathering

Most businesses are run with an eye to specific internal key performance indicators (KPIs), which act as a barometer for output measures such as sales. KPIs differ between industries. For example, in telecommunications, they can be net adds (new subscribers minus lapsed users, or churn) and average revenue per user (ARPU); in financial services, the number of products per customer and their average value to the firm; and in supermarkets, market share, footfall and basket size. These types of measures hint at the underlying drivers of business performance. Third-party analysis of research studies from global research firms such as Nielsen, TGI and Gartner help compare progress with competitors. The overriding principles that marketers should follow when deciding which measures to use and what information and insights need to be gathered are: keep it simple, consistent and commercially focused.

Simple

Do not track too much. Over-frequent measurement of data or too many statistics can be confusing. It is better to have a handful of measures that people really understand than a 20-page dashboard that no one looks at. Tesco's former CEO, Terry Leahy, used a "balanced scorecard" approach, while Michael Dell, founder and CEO of Dell, a computer company, compares monthly cash flow with the currently held stock inventory and adjusts his sales and marketing activities to maximise profits.

Consistent

Aim to get consistency and comparability in data sources, especially when introducing third-party research. Align these with the measures the company uses. Two different sources for market share opens the door to confusion; it is better to decide which one you trust and use it. Where possible, promote consistency across markets and over the longer term for internal measures.

Commercial

Tracking the performance of the marketing department in isolation will do little to demonstrate the contribution to the business's ROI . Many marketing departments scrupulously track traditional marketing or customer-related measures such as awareness, brand consideration, brand equity and customer satisfaction. Yet they are not able to link these to the KPIs that are central to the business.

Investment prioritisation analysis

One of the most useful pieces of initial analysis for marketers in formulating a marketing strategy is a marketing investment prioritisation analysis. This helps to define which markets, products or segments create the most financial value for the company, both now and in the future. One example of this prioritisation method is portfolio analysis (see Chapter 7), which can be used to identify the top seven products in a portfolio of 400 by revenue, profit and brand equity. Portfolio analysis helps make sure that investments are aligned appropriately with value creation. Figure 2.1 shows the investment prioritisation analysis of a global brand, highlighting the strongest five opportunities to increase business performance.

Investment analysis can help with prioritisation of product, market and customer segment opportunities – for example, through the simple matrix developed by Boston Consulting Group (BCG), often simply referred to as the BCG matrix (see Figure 2.2). This plots

FIG 2.1 **Investment prioritisation analysis**

	Market A, %	Market B, %	Market C, %	Market D, %	Market E, %	Market F, %
Current revenues	29	21	12	11	8	5
Profit growth potential (CAGR next 3 years)	4	7	19	16	5	3
Business potential	High revenues		High growth		Low financial performance	
Current brand awareness	89	77	69	64	53	28
Current brand preference	78	72	57	54	37	11
Brand potential	Strong brand performance				Medium brand	Low brand
Overall market prioritisation	First priority				Second priority	Low priority

market share on one axis and market growth on the other. Products or services are put in one of four categories: cash cows, dogs, problem children and stars.

- Stars are high fliers, generating high profits, but require high maintenance. Keeping them at the top of their game involves constant attention and cash, but the hope is that the star will eventually come down to earth as a cash cow rather than a dog.

- Cash cows have high market share, often in a mature industry. They are milked rather than invested in and bring in far more sales and profits than they cost to maintain. If circumstances in the market change dramatically cash cows can turn into dogs, but it is often difficult for a new entrant to seriously threaten an established cash cow. It does happen, however, as Nokia's fall from favour in the mobile phone market has shown. It dominated the market with star products that over time became cash cows for the firm and finally dogs as they were overtaken by smartphones from Apple and Samsung.

FIG 2.2 **BCG business matrix**

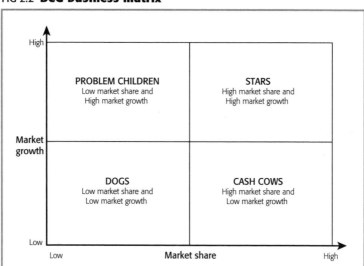

- Dogs are a company's unproductive businesses that lower the return on assets ratio. Investors are not usually happy to let sleeping dogs lie and would prefer them to be sold off or put down.

- Problem children are underperforming in their sector. With time and money it may be possible to convert them into stars, but they are just as likely to turn into dogs, especially if market conditions get tougher.

Prioritisation analysis provides a useful basis for allocating marketing investment. If the analysis classifies the company's products as stars or potential stars, the company's appetite for the investment risk involved must be determined. If it becomes clear that a product is a cash cow, this should help avoid unnecessary spending on marketing activity. For dogs and problem children, the analysis provides the impetus to clean up and reorganise the company's portfolio of products and services.

Linkage to commercial results

It is crucial to decide what data will be the most useful to analyse; in other words, which data will enable marketers to link their strategy and activities directly with commercial outcomes.

Quantitative research will produce data that can be analysed to identify links between marketing activity and business performance. For example, with a TV advertising campaign it is important to gauge how many potential customers are aware of the advertisement and how many of those who are aware are likely to buy the product, and then to cross-reference the results with potential customers who have not seen the advertisement and their likelihood to purchase. From this snapshot a marketer can determine the likely impact on sales and whether it justifies what has been spent on the advertisement. Sales patterns following the campaign can then be compared with what the customer research said was likely to happen. To generate an analysis that really shows how effective an advertisement was, the following factors need to be considered:

- Did the advertisement reach the researched customer group? Was it put out through media channels that the target audience favours? Are there other factors that might influence their decision, such as demographic differences or the fact that they may already own the product?

- Was the sample size of those surveyed representative of the market and large enough to be statistically significant? The ideal is to have at least 100 respondents in each "cell". In this example, a "cell" might be new customers who saw the advertisement and then went out and bought the product. Those surveyed must match the target audience. So if 14% of the target audience for the product are aged 45–65 years, earn above $60,000, live in region X and attitudinally rate product image above price, the research sample needs to have 14% of respondents with those attributes.

Quantitative research provides a sound foundation for rigorous analysis because the data will be current, precisely targeted and can be gathered in a few weeks. Market research agencies are well practised at commissioning and running surveys, but before a firm is briefed the following should be considered:

- Has similar research been done before? What were the findings? What questions should be included in this survey so that the results can be related to previous studies?
- What questions will the directors want answered by the research? What decisions will be taken as a result of the findings? How will the survey answer the board's queries, and will it produce the information in a way that is meaningful to those who have to make or approve the decisions?
- What will suit the purposes of those responsible for marketing?

Consumers do not behave in real life as they do in surveys, but it is possible to design surveys where the answers are likely to be significantly more "right" than "wrong".

Regression analysis

Regression analysis is a much used statistical method of calculating the relationship between independent variables and a single dependent variable. The dependent variable might be sales of the product by month and the independent variables could be spending on advertising, sponsorship, PR and social media by month. For example, it may appear that for each extra 10% a company spends on sponsorship, sales increase by 1%; whereas a 10% increase in advertising spend results in only a 0.5% increase in sales. However, other factors may be influencing sales, such as seasonality or price. Regression analysis allows these independent variables to be taken into account in working out what factors have the most impact on sales. It is a robust statistical tool, but it is only as good as the data that exist for analysis. Furthermore, the analysis is usually carried out using historical data to get a sense of the trend, and therefore the result may not reflect the way the market now behaves. However, the increasing availability of real-time data is overcoming this potential drawback. Regression analysis is most useful for identifying relativities and for range finding – for example, the maximum likely uplift on sales from sponsorship investment. Or it can identify what makes more of a difference to profitability – the amount spent on media or how much more expensive the product is than a competitor's.

Discrete choice modelling

Discrete choice modelling (DCM), sometimes referred to as conjoint or strategic choice analysis, involves potential customers being presented with a choice of products, of which they have to select the one they are most likely to buy. The exercise involves a number of elements: the brand, different product features, different prices and perhaps different distribution channels or service levels. The customer is shown a sequence of product choices that involve different combinations of the various elements. The range of different combinations ensures that they make candid choices that can then be analysed to arrive at the preferred combination of product, price and features for each customer type. This type of research is particularly good for assessing the trade-off that customers make between prices and features. The output is based on two measurement methods:

- The significance of each element compared with others in the buyer's decision-making process (also called the "importance"). For example, if price makes up 30% of the decision, other factors 25% and the brand 45%. This allows marketers to quantify the somewhat intangible brand influence on the customer's choice as well as the more tangible price elements.

- The significance of each element to a purchaser compared with its significance in the case of a competitor's product. For one company, the importance attached to the brand may contribute 45% of the purchase decision, while for a competitor's product it may contribute only 20% of the decision.

DCM helps identify which product features customers are willing to pay more for and which they are not, so it helps businesses maximise profits. If there are many variables to consider, touch point analysis is used to measure the relative importance of different elements of customers' experiences – what marketers call "touch points" – in relation to overall satisfaction. This can be done through standard regression analysis techniques or against price through DCM.

This is in contrast to the purchase funnel (see strategic marketing analytics below), which looks at customers' relationship to the brand over time. Touch point analysis and design is covered in detail in Chapter 9. These techniques are excellent at revealing price elasticity – how flexible customers are about a specific price. It also highlights the potential revenue and margin uplift from introducing different product variants, or which competitor poses the greatest threat if it launches a me-too product.

Data mining current customers

Data mining is a way to derive insights about customers' needs and behaviour from the data held about them and their purchases. This can then be used to devise products and services that are more tailored to them. It helps bridge the gap between qualitative research – the "why" – and real-world analytics – the "what".

Integrating transactional sales "big data" with the wider customer information available online through both e-commerce and social-media platforms provides a much richer seam of information for the marketer to work with in terms of personalisation, cross-selling and a host of tools to increase advocacy of products, brands and customer lifetime value. According to McKinsey, a consulting firm, which has done extensive research into data mining:

> A retailer using big data to the full could increase its operating margin by more than 60%. If US healthcare were to use big data creatively and effectively the sector could create more than $300 billion in value every year.

The 2011 IBM Global CMO Study revealed that marketers are now waking up to the potential of data mining:

> Companies currently spend an average of 5.7% of their marketing budgets on marketing analytics and this number is expected to grow to 9.1% in the next three years. Marketing budgets overall have grown 8.3% over the last two years. Services companies overall spend more on marketing analytics now and will remain ahead of product companies in the next three years. Service companies

appear to understand the big data opportunity and believe they can leverage it to create more value for their customers.

Big data allows service brands to develop "mass customisation" where either the product or the experience can to some degree be personalised – if not to individual customers, then to segments who then have a sense of their individual needs being met. Dell is famous for leading the way in this. In the fast-moving consumer goods (FMCG) sector, the understanding of customer segments and regional trends allows mass-market producers to tailor offers that appear to answer individual customer needs. In the online environment, it permits the creation of algorithms to deliver targeted advertising across web browsing. Above all, it is the cornerstone of customer relationship management.

Scenario planning

It is important that any research data provides good insights to inform future strategy. These insights can be tested in scenario planning exercises. At a simple level this might involve "what would you need to believe" analysis, which turns the traditional research question on its head and asks "what conditions would need to be true for X to be a good idea"? For example, a consumer goods company might hypothesise that:

■ there is sufficient commonality of customer needs and perceptions to warrant a single master brand strategy;

■ the master brand will outperform the family of sub-brands in driving customer preference and choice in most markets.

Different scenarios will have different strengths and weaknesses. One scenario may offer higher rewards with higher investment costs and risks, while another may offer lower returns with lower risks. But the exercise enables strategy and plans to be shaped according to the most credible hypotheses and most likely scenario in order to achieve the optimum outcome. For example, choosing a single master brand strategy for every market may yield higher average returns overall but some individual markets may deliver above or below average returns. Scenario planning allows management teams to test what might happen if a particular strategy is chosen before investing time and energy in it and without the risk of actually implementing the strategy.

EBITDA bridge

A much used measure, or target, is the earnings before interest, taxes, depreciation and amortisation (EBITDA) bridge. This is a projection of the EBITDA figure for the year ahead that takes into account future sales, product launches and other factors or assumptions about the business and allows for a margin of error. This sets financial goals such as an X% increase in new sales and a Y% increase in sales to current customers or markets. The marketing team can then give thought to what activities and overall marketing strategy are most likely to help achieve those financial goals. Figure 2.3 illustrates the EBITDA bridge based on Lloyds Banking Group's 2011 strategic review with potential marketing actions.

FIG 2.3 **An EBITDA bridge**

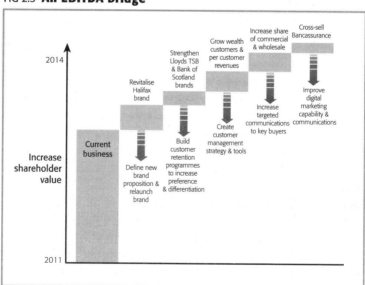

Source: Lloyds Banking Group Strategic Review, 2011

Strategic marketing analytics

In first three stages of information gathering and analysis, insight gathering determines what kind of information is required to drive marketing performance; investment prioritisation analysis determines marketing strategy priorities; and linkage to commercial results places marketing activities in a financial context that the board can understand. The fourth stage, strategic marketing analytics, involves specific techniques for improving brand and marketing performance; it helps firms identify growth opportunities and the marketing strategies that will make the most of them.

Purchase funnel analysis

This process tracks the consumer's journey towards the purchase of a product or service. It typically has five main components:

- awareness of the product;
- consideration of the product for purchase;
- preference of the product against other products;
- purchase of the product;
- becoming a positive advocate for the product.

Figure 2.4 gives an example of a purchase funnel showing conversion ratios across each stage.

The purchase funnel helps identify at which stage potential customers are being lost and therefore where to focus investment. It can also help estimate the expected potential financial returns. There are several ways to use the purchase funnel.

A funnel must reflect the brand and category, and so how the five elements of awareness, consideration, preference, purchase and advocacy fit consumer touch points, such as advertising, direct mail and peer influence, must be clearly defined. Then the stages of the funnel at which people are drawn to or leave the brand need to be identified. Typically, as seen in Figure 2.4, more and more people lose interest in a particular brand as they progress down the funnel, and so it is the element within the funnel that is causing the greatest drop in numbers that most needs to be addressed.

FIG 2.4 **A consumer purchase funnel**

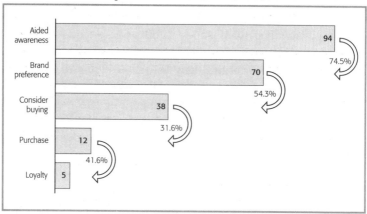

Next, key performance indicators should be defined that are relevant to each stage, with particular regard to the stages at which there is the greatest fall-off in consumer interest. For example, a large number of consumers will consider the brand but significantly fewer indicate a preference for it in research. This indicates that awareness is not the issue and that some kind of promotional activity or a campaign to increase advocacy of the brand is needed to increase the number of people choosing it instead of another. Lastly, a financial value should be attributed to the different elements of the funnel. Rather than looking at the percentage of customers lost or retained, it is more useful to assess the financial value lost or retained. If the funnel ends at purchase or acquisition, this will be average revenue, profit per customer or lifetime value. Further valuable insight can be gained from examining post-purchase measures such as satisfied versus unsatisfied customers or repeat purchasers versus churners. The purchase funnel can be used in scenarios to model the impact on value from different scenarios, such as closing the gap on awareness against a competitor, and against a 5% increase in satisfied customers. If it is possible to factor in the cost of making the change to get an estimated ROI, this will be even better.

Valuation of intangible brand assets

It is now common for companies with well-known brands to put a value on these intangible assets on their balance sheets. This has coincided with a marked reduction in the size of companies' tangible assets, as economies become dominated by services and companies that own valuable patents or trademark brands. There are several brand valuation indices produced by brand consultancies such as Brand Finance, BrandZ (Millward Brown) and Interbrand. The building blocks of these valuation approaches are similar. They are based on:

■ analysis of financial performance and a forecast of revenues or profits, discounted to current value;

■ quantitative research that enables an assessment to be made in order to arrive at the contribution of the brand to those revenues/profits, as opposed to the contribution of other factors such as price or product features;

■ a subjective assessment of the strength of the brand – allowance should be made for the possibility that the future revenues are not achieved.

Of these three building blocks, the performance forecast is given by far the heaviest weighting.

Brand Finance

■ Calculates the future revenues (as opposed to profits) attributable to the brand over a five-year forecast period.

■ Assesses the brand strength using its BrandBeta index. This index adopts the creditworthiness approach of ratings agencies Standard & Poor's (S&P) or Moody's and rates the brand from AAA (extremely strong) down to DDD (failing). The rating is based on company annual reports and Brand Finance research.

■ Applies the average royalty rate for the relevant sector. A royalty rate is used as a proxy for the value of using a brand on an unbranded product. For example, if a company were to license a brand for its product, it would cost $X. This rule-of-thumb approach avoids the need for detailed financial analysis of the brand contribution. Royalty rates are based on comparable licensing agreements – similar to the brand contribution factor calculated by Interbrand and BrandZ. The royalty rate is multiplied by the BrandBeta index to determine the brand-specific royalty rate.

- Determines the discount rate using discounted cash flow (DCF) methodology and subtracts tax to obtain the NPV of royalty rates.

Millward Brown: BrandZ

- Calculates company earnings generated under the banner of the brand, net of capital charges. Only current earnings are used, rather than the five-year DCF.

- Calculates the proportion of this value that is attributable to the brand alone (the brand contribution). This contribution is based on country, market and brand-specific customer research in Millward Brown's proprietary brand tracking database so it may differ slightly from the brand contribution values applied by other brand consultancies, although industry relativities will be the same.

- Scores the short-term growth potential of the branded earnings – the brand momentum (BM) – out of 10. This is an index of the growth rate against the competition and takes into account the likelihood of an increase in market share. It is a relative measure of how efficiently a brand is able to convert people who are considering a product to actually purchase it and therefore the likelihood that company sales will increase. The concept of BM is a combination of two stages in the Interbrand approach:
  - the calculation of the five-year DCF rather than current earnings;
  - the brand risk discount factor – the brand-driven value is multiplied by the BM score out of 10 to generate an expected earnings multiple.

Interbrand

■ Uses the shareholder value creation method (discussed earlier) to calculate the NPV (based on a company's five-year future cash flow forecast).

■ Calculates the proportion of this value that is attributable to the brand itself, often based on expert opinion or shopper research that measures what proportion of a customer's buying decision is attributable to the brand relative to other factors such as price or features. It scores the quality of brand management out of 100. This is a cumulative score derived from the scores of ten factors of brand management, worth ten points for each.

■ Applies a discount factor to the brand-driven value based on the brand-management score. This attempts to account for brand risk – the risk that the brand may decline in value as a result of, say, poor management or more effective competitors. The higher the brand-management score, the lower the risk; hence the lower the discount factor.

The main structural differences in the three approaches (apart from the technical details of how the profit forecast and brand contribution are assessed) are in assessing brand strength and selecting the brands on the list. Assessing brand strength is the most subjective of the valuation elements, though frameworks and external customer research are used to add rigour to the evaluations. Brand Finance uses investor sources like Moody's for its assessment. In selecting its brands, Millward Brown's BrandZ ranking starts afresh each year with a list of the top 100 brands based on consumer awareness from its brand tracking research. Interbrand's ranking is based more on the previous year's list with selected additions and removals. As a result, it shows more consistency between years but arguably contains anachronistic brand survivors.

The ideal brand valuation would blend high-quality quantitative research into customers with expert analysis of financial and management performance. This would help connect the different customer perceptions of a brand with its equity (or value). The perceptions of a brand will vary at least to some extent geographically and culturally, and so its global equity reflects the total value those different perceptions underpin.

Customer relationship management

Tesco, one of the world's largest supermarket groups, has a Clubcard loyalty scheme. It is an example of how useful customer data mining can be in increasing sales per customer and customer loyalty, as well as helping in the development of new products and promotional propositions. In an effort to mine the data from the millions of customers that shop at its stores, Tesco created its own data-mining agency, DunnHumby, which uses an algorithmic approach that correlates price promotions with customer buying patterns to make sure that offers are attractive and encourage consumers to increase their basket size, whether in-store or online. For the retailer, data mining delivers hard facts on which to base negotiations with suppliers and informs future merchandising strategies. It is this tangible proof of customer behaviour that makes all the difference in influencing corporate strategy.

Integrating comprehensive data mining into customer management processes is not simple. There are several barriers, mainly from an IT systems perspective:

■ no single customer view – customer data are spread across multiple systems and geographies which do not talk to one another;

■ heavy investment costs – changes may need to be made from transactional point of sale (POS) technologies throughout operations to back-end fulfilment systems;

■ data issues – customer information may be held by third parties, who may not be willing to share, or will charge a lot for doing so;

■ data protection policies – these are often stringent and differ across markets.

Big data is becoming an increasingly powerful weapon in the pursuit of competitive advantage. The longer firms delay investment in sufficiently sophisticated data-mining systems, the harder it will be to catch up with competitors. However, pilot testing with data can deliver top-line insights that both justify further investment in data mining and give marketing the foundational findings to shape strategy. Using third parties can also help a business carry out data-mining projects swiftly while it continues to build its own proprietary solution.

Advocacy analysis

Customer advocacy is an important measure in that it helps identify ways to improve customer value and profitability. Net promoter score – the degree to which customers speak positively of a brand – is one of the best-known advocacy measures. The theory is that companies can use their scores to identify ways to improve customer service, predict growth and decide compensation levels for top-level managers. The score is based on a simple survey of up to 11 points, but is often reduced to three simple categories: promoters, passives and detractors. The maximum index is +/–100. An NPS of –100 is as bad as it gets: every customer is a detractor. An NPS of +100 is perfect: no one has a single bad thing to say about the brand, nor is anyone passive about it; all customers are 100% actively saying positive things about it. In general, an NPS of +50 is considered excellent. Figure 2.5 gives an example of an NPS scale.

The NPS system was devised by Fred Reichfield, a partner at Bain & Co, a consultancy, and SatMetrix, a research company, and explained in a 2003 *Harvard Business Review* article, "One Number You Need to Grow". Supporters of NPS believe that customers are likely to be more discriminatory when asked to rate their "likelihood

FIG 2.5 **NPS scoring system**

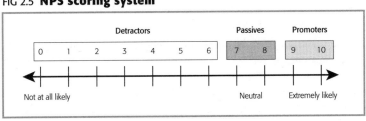

Sources: Satmetrix; Fred Reichfeld; Bain & Company

to recommend" rather than simply general satisfaction. It is also thought that companies will be more likely to change their strategy when faced with a negative NPS rather than a vague customer-satisfaction rating of below 70%. Apple uses NPS scores to constantly monitor and improve its in-store experience. Each Apple store gets an update first thing in the morning of the previous day's scores, along with any issues identified, so that improvements can be immediately implemented. Procter & Gamble uses NPS to measure customer reaction to its brands and General Electric uses it to assess customer service.

NPS does, however, have its detractors. The primary criticism is that while marketers make the distinction between satisfaction and advocacy, consumers when answering the survey generally do not, so the NPS results rather than being distinct from customer satisfaction rates actually mirror them. Another problem is the variability of the NPS depending on industry segment, because whether a business is involved in tobacco or toys is likely to influence consumers' likelihood to recommend. Cultural mores may also affect the NPS of an identical product or service across territories. For example, green "eco" vehicles are highly regarded in countries like Germany but less so in oil-rich countries like Saudi Arabia or Russia. Furthermore, the scoring scale is not evenly distributed, as there is no distinction made between a score of 0 and a score of 6. Both are considered detractors, whereas in most ten-point scoring scales there would be a significantly different interpretation of a 6 score and a zero score.

NPS's main benefit is that it is well recognised and easy to communicate across an organisation. Externally, it is a consistent measure by which to benchmark a brand with competitors and other industries.

Media effectiveness planning

Spending on media is by far the largest part of any marketing budget, often running to billions of dollars for brands like Samsung and American Express. The number of media platforms has also increased and there has been a shift from big-spending broadcast campaigns towards multi-channel targeted media communications. This has put pressure on marketers to make sure that their budget is spent wisely and efficiently. Media platforms are not simply competing among themselves for a slice of the pie but with alternative methods such as CRM-based direct marketing. Media strategy is covered in more detail Chapter 9, but the main measures used in the pursuit of getting the right message to the right customer at the right time as cost-effectively as possible are as follows:

- **Reach** – the percentage of customers or households that need to be exposed to advertising during a campaign. A "reach curve" is the industry term for how the number of distinct individuals or households changes with increased exposure to different media types. For example, some households will see an advertisement many times, so the curve will start converging on a maximum possible reach, equivalent to the percentage of target customers who ever watch the channel.

- **Frequency** – the number of times customers or households should be exposed to the message. One rule of thumb used in advertising in above the line (ATL) media such as television or radio is that customers need to see an advertisement three times before they feel compelled to act.

- **Cost** – in print media, measured in cost per thousand (CPM), the cost of the advert against its circulation in thousands; in broadcast media, measured in cost per point, the cost of reaching 1% of the target audience; in below the line (BTL) activities such as direct mail phone calls, e-mail or SMS, measured in cost per contact.

- **Return on investment** – or the expected sales or profit uplift from the media channel exposure. This may be based on previous campaigns or trials or quantitative research.

Media plans often stop at outputs, such as reach and frequency targets versus cost, rather than business outcomes. A media-spend analysis can be used to trade off these four measures to reveal the most effective one.

After the event, media campaigns are measured on a few dimensions, such as cut through (the percentage being aware of the campaign or advertisement multiplied by the percentage associating it with the brand), and specific attributes, such as the extent to which the campaign communicated the brand attributes to consumers.

A future of big data and real-time analytics

Big data will unlock rich opportunities for the firms that manage it cleverly. It is the next big battleground for competitive advantage for marketers and their organisations. A 2012 Harvard Business School study, "Big Data: The management revolution", of over 300 US listed companies identified that those making use of data-driven decisions were on average 5% more productive and 6% more profitable than competitors that were not doing so. The transformational shift towards real-time data is driven by technological advances, particularly cloud-based computer storage, the effectiveness of database analytics programmes and the opening up of new direct channels, such as websites, social media and mobile data, which can be more easily tracked. However, nearly three-quarters (71%) of the executives who took part in the 2011 IBM Global CMO Study said they did not feel ready to take advantage of the real-time data revolution. Businesses that do not want to get left behind need to focus particularly on what the most effective types of data are and how to improve predictions through increased speed and variety.

The new digital era, covered in more detail in Chapter 9, increases speed of information flow and word of mouth and makes it harder (sometimes almost impossible) for marketers to control the impact on customers. The essential channels to master in real-time data are as follows:

- **Website analytics.** The company or brand's website ranking, such as number of visitors, source of visit and subsequent departure point, from analytics brands like Alexa or Hitwise; website engagement quality (composite index of percentage of returning visitors, dwell time on site, pages viewed, bounce rate), available from Google Analytics; conversion funnels and usage paths, available from Google Analytics (what paths do customers take through the site, which pages are most and least popular, where do they drop off); search statistics (key words, referring traffic, upstream and downstream).

■ **Attribution modelling.** Software such as doubleclick or DC-storm can be used to track customers viewing an online advert, for example pay per click (PPC) or banner ad, and through cookies identify whether they later visit the site or buy a product, enabling tracking of advertising effectiveness.

■ **Social media.** Social-media "buzz", such as mentions on chat forums, "likes" on Facebook, tweets on Twitter, connections on LinkedIn; verbal analysis software to automatically scan through the contents of social-networking references to the company and summarise key themes. Procter & Gamble is hooking up its product teams to a live feed of blog posts about the products. The rule of thumb is to focus on Facebook first and then crack Twitter.

■ **Mobile data and near-field communications.** Mobile phone-based data that helps to understand customers and their location-based browsing and purchasing behaviour – and could be, for example, used to e-mail customers a discount voucher when they are close to a store.

The biggest challenge for marketers is how to decide which data will unlock the most value. Building huge data banks of detailed information might seem to be the answer, but smart firms are increasingly analysing real-time data from a variety of sources to make rapid predictions that can be used to fine tune their marketing tactics every week, day or even hour. This "velocity" model has proved just as effective as much more costly and complex systems. For example, a group of MIT researchers used the location-based data from customers' mobile phones to identify how many people parked in a Macy's store car park on the busiest shopping day of the year. They could then estimate, with other publicly available data, the retailer's sales on that day before the store closed. This kind of insight is far more valuable (and perishable) than the backward-looking log of actual sales that management received a few days later. Although it is important, this historical record cannot influence actual sales.

The velocity approach to prediction is accurate enough and, crucially, recent enough that management can take action to change the outcome of the day's sales. Marketers can use their customer knowledge to identify approaches that increase the velocity of analysis and insight over absolute volumes of historical data.

As with building segmentation models, building optimal analytics models relies on the creativity of the inputs. There is a lot of data out there but finding interesting and meaningful ways to link a variety of data sets, not just the volumes of data analysed, is where the value creation happens. Linking data on the life stages of customers with online shopping basket analysis can help predict when couples are likely to have babies in a particular neighbourhood and when they require essential baby products so that a store can increase its stocks. Another retail brand might link weather-pattern predictions to increased sales in good weather. Pinterest, a content-sharing service that allows members to "pin" images and videos to their pinboard, helps customers be aware of trends such as an increase in the popularity of Japanese food. This will help retailers identify peaks in demand for Japanese cooking utensils like sushi trays or chopsticks and adjust stocks and staff training accordingly.

It is essential that marketers look beyond their own firm's data for insights rather than simply squeezing their historical purchase data harder for little gain. These changes in use of real-time data mean that marketers need to adapt their thinking and management style. There are opportunities to transform business processes in most industries, but this requires decision-making at the point of the most up-to-date information rather than the highest point in the management hierarchy. This means that frontline employees and data scientists become the leading insight generators of growth opportunities for businesses. The task for marketers is to help lead change through the use of rigorous analytics of customer needs, motivation and behaviour and the factors that influence these three aspects.

Summary

The rapid growth in the availability of data, both historic and real-time, on customers' behaviour and preferences provides marketers with more accurate forecasting tools. They can use these to better analyse and help predict more effective product features, pricing and marketing promotion activities. This shift from decisions made largely on intuition to a strategy built on more rigorous analysis aligns the marketing function more closely with other functional areas that have routinely used statistically robust fact-based decision-making. The use of real-time data presents both a challenge to understand the volumes of big data available and an opportunity to fine tune marketing promotions more closely to individual needs and preferences. This requires marketing teams to gain new skills in data capture, analysis and interpretation.

3 Barriers to growth

LINKING MARKETING'S CONTRIBUTION analytically to commercial results is critical in helping business growth and in demonstrating that the marketing function produces more than just intangible benefits as a result of decisions made on the basis of gut feeling. Yet the psychology of human decision-making should never be ignored. Managers may in public claim that a strategic decision is based on empirical evidence; in private, however, they may be more willing to admit the role of intuition in their decisions. There are in effect two brain systems that control our decision-making: one, the limbic part of the brain, operates swiftly and automatically with no sense of voluntary control and is thus open to situational biases and errors; the other, the neo-cortex, is deductive and controlled but requires conscious motivation to be activated and is slower to reach decisions. Managers need to be aware of the way the brain works when making decisions.

This chapter explores the thinking or cognitive biases that affect business decision-making and may have the effect of constraining a business's growth. The four main obstacles to effective decision-making are:

■ cognitive ease;
■ loss aversion;
■ representativeness;
■ anchoring the value of a brand.

Cognitive ease

In a world where decisions have to be made with imperfect, limited information under time pressure, human decision-making has developed shortcuts for judging the believability of any piece of information. Decision scientists call this cognitive ease or fluency. Put simply, cognitive ease or fluency is how easy the brain finds it to process a piece a piece of information. People naturally prefer things that are cognitively easy rather than demanding, but this preference can result in erroneous decisions. Cognitive ease helps explain real-world puzzles such as why people are more likely to invest in companies with easy-to-pronounce names.

The cognitively easy message here is that the simpler and more believable a business case is, the more likely it is to get approval; in other words, a chief executive is more likely to be swayed in support of a marketing proposal by three clear reasons than ten complicated ones.

Use plain business English

Marketers like other professionals have a habit of creating their own vocabulary partly to give a sense of mystique or exclusivity to what they do. But marketing-speak simply creates barriers between them and their non-marketing colleagues, in the same way that legal-speak can create a barrier between lawyers and their clients. Managers today already use far too much jargon, so the more everyone in a company speaks the same plain business English the better they will all understand each other – and therefore the better the reasons for making a decision will be understood.

At Zingerman, a community-based American catering business, employees talk about customer satisfaction in terms of "number of meals sent back to the kitchen". This is both a tangible figure and a direct representation of satisfaction, not an abstract, high-level measure of customer happiness. By simplifying the measures that are reported to the board and the way marketing concepts are discussed within a company, everyone from frontline staff to the directors can understand what is going on in the business and contribute to improving performance. The net promoter score (see Chapter 2) is a good measure that marketers should understand and use, but when talking to the rest of the organisation simple, clear language is what wins the day. It would be simpler to say that more customers like the brand than do not like it.

Loss aversion

"Losses loom larger than corresponding gains," says Daniel Kahneman, a Nobel prize-winning psychologist, in his book *Thinking Fast and Slow.*

Loss aversion is a person's belief that losses are perceived as far greater in their mind than the equivalent gains. This results in an overly cautious outlook for businesses. If a company attempts to change customers' buying patterns there is potential for gain, but there is also the risk that they might be turned off the brand. Loss aversion can stifle change and growth.

Loss aversion was first convincingly described by Kahneman and Amos Tversky in their 1979 paper, *Prospect Theory, Analysis of Decision Under Risk.* They suggested that losses have twice the psychological impact as similar gains during decision-making. For customers, this means that they weigh losses much more than gains based on a perceived reference point. If their favourite beer brand is unavailable in a bar and they choose another, more expensive brand, the reference point is their favourite beer. According to loss aversion theory, the customers are likely to worry about the additional expense rather than relishing the finer-tasting beer. The loss is magnified more than the gain. Equally, if they choose a cheaper beer than their usual one, the perceived poorer taste will be magnified to a greater extent than the money saving. Thus customers do not perceive losses and gains equally.

Brand switching and loss aversion

Loss aversion among customers is the biggest challenge faced by marketers in persuading customers to switch to a different brand. Customers will use their current preferred brand as the reference point for judging any potential substitute. They will emphasise any potential loss of product quality over any gain. The new brand will have to be significantly better on one or two brand attributes to overcome customer loss aversion if the price points are similar or even slightly favour the new variant. If the products are largely identical, any other incentive to switch such as price will have to be at least twice as enticing. But embarking on a price discounting strategy to win over customers is likely to provoke retaliation and may well lock those competing brands into systemic value destruction rather than sustainable value creation.

Loss aversion in customers can be based on almost perversely small aspects. Customer mobility – the willingness to switch brands – in the premium vodka category is incredibly low. In 2012 Grey Goose, a Bacardi-owned premium vodka brand, was ranked the 14th most loyal brand in any category by Brand Keys, a brand research consultancy. Yet the potential for disappointment in changing brands is minimal; the product itself is a near colourless and tasteless alcohol. However, customers are strikingly loyal to their Vodka brand, with Belvedere, Ketel One and Grey Goose each having its own cult following.

Loss aversion can be so strong that a customer is unwilling to spend even a small amount on testing an alternative. It should be easy for customers to understand which product features are similar to the competition and which are different, enabling them to trade off potential losses and gains effectively. The topic of points of similarity and points of differentiation among products is covered in more detail in Chapter 5.

Reducing the fear of loss

To gain new customers, marketers need to be clear which attributes or benefits the target segment fears losing most. These may or may not be the same attributes they desire most – an important distinction. Deprivation research is a good way to understand the priority given to potential losses. It involves taking a product away from customers for a set time and asking them to keep a diary of how they feel without that product. A 2011 survey by Telenav, an American provider of navigation services, highlighted that 70% of women would rather give up sex for a week than their mobile phones. Deprivation research can identify the benefits that those customers fear losing most.

Some marketing managers have managed customers' fears well. Just after the financial crises of 2008, car manufacturers slashed their prices to appeal to both price-conscious and loss-averse customers. Hyundai recognised customers' biggest fear of the moment – lack of job security – and entered the market with a reassuring message, promising that customers could return their cars if they lost their jobs in the year following the purchase. In just a month, American sales rose by 20%; according to Martin Lindstrom, the author of *Buyology: How Everything We Believe About Why We Buy is Wrong*, apparently only two cars were returned.

Loss aversion is likely to be stronger in highly competitive sectors. For example, price-comparison websites have encouraged insurance firms to compete almost solely on price, though research has shown that provided you are in the top five for price, it is brand recognition that matters in consumer choice rather than price. However, there are signs that a growing number of firms are choosing not to join the race to the bottom on price and are refusing to allow their products to be featured on price-comparison websites. Direct Line, a UK pioneer in selling insurance direct, is notable for its absence on these websites, preferring to put resources into driving people to its own contact centres. It was a bold marketing choice to run counter to the loss aversion strategy followed by other insurance firms, but it has paid off in consolidating the company's position among UK insurers as the number two brand. By not using comparison sites, Direct Line avoids the customer reference point of the cheapest insurance quote. Without that reference, it is much easier for Direct Line to sell based on its own distinct customer benefits. It is more in control of the rules of the game and therefore of increasing its competitive advantage.

Boldly going

Marketers are by nature optimists because their main task is demand creation for their products. But they are also wary of failure. Given the choice between incrementally improving a service with a high likelihood of success and a groundbreaking improvement with a bigger risk of failure, they will typically avoid the latter. This is why so many products and services are good but not great. Marketers, like many people, avoid potential losses too easily, even if the data suggest little risk. To do something different in the marketplace requires courage and commitment.

Steve Jobs of Apple lacked the loss aversion characteristic. He rarely avoided trying something new and this led to the immensely successful iPhone smartphone and iPad tablet, spawning a host of me-too brands competing ferociously for market share. He was a visionary who had an intuitive sense for what consumers wanted and an in-depth understanding of how to improve their experience of technology. Apple is a company that has shown it can lead by being bold, but also what happens when it becomes more conservative. Its incremental refinements of its iPhone product have merely kept pace with the competition, and in some areas it has fallen behind competitors like Samsung and Google.

Most companies whose products or services undergo only incremental improvements will probably experience a reduction in consumer preference for their brand. But the disadvantages of loss aversion can be overcome by being bolder. Bold decisions are no more (and can be much less) risky than loss-aversion-influenced decisions, providing they are clearly thought through and focus on producing the greatest revenues and profit in the longer term rather than minimising the shorter-term potential financial downside.

Extending the brand

Brand extension can form one part of a growth strategy. Businesses that control well-known brands often like to see if they can extend their appeal beyond the products they are associated with. The assumption is that existing customers will also buy the variant extension thus increasing basket size, and that new customers will be acquired as these new products, with a trusted brand pedigree, address a new segment's needs. However, while extending or stretching the brand into new products and even new categories of goods can contribute to growth, the strategy sometimes backfires, as Bic discovered.

Bic, a company that became famous for its disposable pens, extended its brand successfully into lighters and pens, which shared the same core attributes of functionality, disposability, affordability and easily identifiable styling. Bic then ventured into underwear, which was a disaster. It turned out that people did not want to buy ladies underwear from a brand that is associated with blades, points and flames and has a logo of a small orange-suited man carrying what looks like a black lance.

Bic's failure suggests poor analysis of the opportunity. There may be space in the market for inexpensive but well-made and functional underwear, and customers are now aware that recycled plastic products, perhaps including pens and razor handles, are used to make synthetic clothing. However, this does not mean the customer wants a maker of pens and razors to make lingerie.

The representativeness rule of thumb

Representativeness is often used as a rule of thumb to judge the likely success of a brand extension based on others' previous experiences. There may appear to be no reason for a business that is capable of providing well-made cheap underwear not to do so, but whether people will buy Bic underwear will depend to a large extent on whether the brand seems representative of underwear. Bic may have been encouraged to venture into clothing by the success of Caterpillar, a maker of diggers and heavy machinery, in stretching its brand to footwear, including women's sandals. But Caterpillar's extension into women's sandals makes sense because it was another step in a carefully staged journey of extensions for the brand. From industrial diggers, the company extended first into metal-tipped work boots – essential for any worker manning such machinery. As is often the case, work boots were worn outside the building site and became desirable footwear for anyone who needed strong foot protection or simply liked the styling of a heavy-duty boot. As Caterpillar became known for high-quality functional footwear, the proposition was re-engineered for a more mainstream market and then as a natural extension into the functional women's wear market. This is why it makes sense to customers that an industrial digger brand can make women's footwear. Bic's adventure into underwear turned out to be too big a stretch for the brand – at least in one leap.

Harley Davidson, a motorcycle manufacturer, similarly used a rule of thumb in its development of a Harley Davidson fragrance. It probably reviewed hundreds of examples of fragrance brands born out of brand extensions. Ralph Lauren is almost as famous for its expensive scents as it is for fashion clothing. Footballers such as David Beckham have a range of scents, and even football clubs sell aftershave. Caterpillar sells a fragrance product and Ferrari has a large range of branded products including aftershave. It is easy to understand how these brands led the marketers at Harley Davidson to believe that they too could succeed with their own scent product.

For Harley Davidson, the rule of thumb proved inaccurate as its fragrance tanked in the marketplace. It mistook a rule of thumb for true representativeness of its specific customers and market. In this case, most mainstream Harley Davidson customers are comfortably off senior managers who ride sedately at weekends and wear Ralph Lauren, even under their leathers. And if they wear Ralph Lauren, it is more than likely they wear that scent too.

How brands make decision-making easier

Without detailed analysis of technical performance figures, dimensions and driving experiences, brands themselves help customers make choices that involve complex trade-offs. It is easy enough for people to understand that the BMW 5 Series car is better than a BMW 3 Series car and is in many respects similar to a Lexus GS 350 car.

Brands and their sub-brands become the rule of thumb that is accurate enough for customers to make a broad decision about which car brand they want to buy. This is both the strength and weakness of rules of thumb; they work extremely well for a directional judgment but not for a specific one, because rules of thumb are not accurately representative. Broadly, both are premium executive cars but they attract different types of customers and deliver the experience in different ways. BMW focuses on the product and driving experience, while Lexus focuses on the reliability and service aspects of the brand – therefore they are clearly not the same. Marketers need to assess at what level of generalisation they can use a rule of thumb and when detailed analysis is essential.

In their simplest sense, brands provide a safe option. When swamped with choice or even a necessity for action, such as an insurance renewal date, customers are more likely choose the brand they have used before rather than switch, even if their motivation for doing so to avoid nasty surprises.

Getting to grips with the customer

Customer targeting is discussed further in Chapter 4, which describes how data and insights can help companies get more value from customers. Simple fact-based analysis of customer research provides an accurate foundation for making marketing investment decisions. Customer value and profitability analysis must be methodical to ensure accuracy and to enable marketing activity to be tailored and targeted to best effect at, say, specific customer segments or individual customers with distinct characteristics.

Expensive and time-consuming research into a large number of customer segments is often not necessary. A high-level study to identify four or five profitable customer segments followed by a detailed study of one or two customer groups may be much more cost effective and quicker. For example, an airline might use its loyalty programme to identify its highest and average value customers, and then carry out a detailed study of those two groups to establish any significant differences in their needs, behaviours and drivers of value. One airline that did this found that the drivers of value among both groups were more similar than anticipated. On-board attention and care mattered to all, but the style and level of that care differed greatly between the groups. This led the airline to focus on building a single competitive capability for its brand based on care which it then executed differently across cabin classes. By focusing on a single capability it gained efficiency, and by offering it to both customer groups, albeit in different styles, it increased the likelihood of upgrades from one cabin to the next. This increased customer profitability and longer-term customer value.

Anchoring the value of a brand

Choosing the right frame of reference or anchor is essential when making decisions related to a brand. In a classic research experiment, two groups of participants were asked to estimate the number of

African countries that were members of the United Nations. Before the question was posed, each group of participants was in passing given the atomic weight of a chemical element, one a high number and the other a low one. Those given the high number estimated a much higher number of African countries than those given the low one. The irrelevant information they had been given about atomic weights had acted as a reference point – or anchor – for their answers.

De Beers' "A diamond is forever" campaign is one of the most successful examples of a marketing anchor based on a customer need. Despite the fact that diamonds can be destroyed and chipped and can change colour, the idea of a diamond being the most long lasting of the gemstones is ingrained in popular belief. However, until the 1930s demand for diamonds was low and they were changing hands at much lower prices than the equivalent today. It was only after a publicity onslaught in the United States in the 1940s involving lectures and mass advertising featuring Hollywood stars that a diamond engagement ring became the thing to be seen with.

De Beers continues to reframe the relevance of its product for each new generation. In the 1990s it persuaded many male customers to spend more on engagement rings by anchoring the decision-making reference point to a price point that represented three months of an average middle-class person's salary. "What else can your salary buy that will last forever?" the tagline questioned. According to company insiders, customers who knew and used the guideline spent an average of 30% more on an engagement ring than those who had not heard this message. Not surprisingly, other jewellery sellers quickly copied the idea. De Beers has recently started targeting women as its primary customers. Advertisements suggest women should show off their independence and success by displaying the diamond rings they bought for themselves on their right hand.

Summary

Customer and corporate psychology may seem unlikely tools for taking concrete business decisions. But as it is individuals who interpret research data and take these decisions, it is important to understand the influence of cognitive thinking processes on those concrete outcomes. Often the barrier to improvement is not the data but the interpretation of it, or a reluctance to take the bold decisions inferred by this new knowledge. Understanding the likely biases of individuals can help companies avoid deep-rooted but wrong assumptions and rules of thumb. The psychological frameworks covered in this chapter should help managers to avoid some of the human bias in their decision-making that may form barriers to company growth.

4 Targeting customers and external stakeholders

A 2011 IBM SURVEY found that over 75% of chief marketing officers (CMOs) felt they had significant influence over promotion, the first "P" in the four Ps of marketing, as described by E. Jerome McCarthy. But fewer than half of those surveyed felt they had significant influence over the other three Ps: product, place and price. Customer targeting and segmentation allows marketers to expand their influence beyond the confines of advertising, sales and promotion. Linking segmentation and targeting effectively to customer value management leads to marketing-driven growth – and boosts marketers' credibility and influence in the boardroom.

Better customer targeting will increase revenues and enable marketers to:

■ increase sales and profits through increased attraction, relevance and differentiation of propositions;

■ gain and serve customers quicker and better though smarter segmentation and customer engagement;

■ build strong brands that transcend and reinforce individual products and service benefits;

■ build loyalty with customers and increase the robustness of the brand and any other brands and sub-brands in the portfolio to stabilise risks.

It comes down to being clear about which specific customer groups might buy the product, what their needs and purchase behaviours are, and adapting the offer to them accordingly. It means being clear about which groups of customers companies want to encourage to buy their products and which they do not, and getting a fair share of those not directly targeted but who still buy the products or services. Targeting is really about setting priorities.

Defining the customer target

Customer targeting helps marketers identify the most profitable avenues for future growth and expansion and can reveal category-defining changes that catapult brands to the top of the pile. Most customer analysis focuses on segmentation and measuring brand perceptions. Segmentation is the process of subdividing the market into specific groups of customers that may share needs, attitudes or the way they use or buy a product. This process allows marketers to select the most attractive customer segment to focus on. Zara, a Spanish fashion brand, has a clear target audience (see Figure 4.1) and everything Zara does is designed to satisfy it.

Zara's competitive advantage is based on its ability to produce a fast-changing range of fashionable garments and getting them into its stores quickly at low cost. The company can design, produce, distribute and put a garment on display in any of its stores worldwide in a mere 15 days because it produces around 50% of the garments in its own factories around the world. This is unusual in this clothing

FIG 4.1 **Zara customer profile**

Demographics	18–30 years old
	Degree-level education
	Predominantly female
	50% have children
	$30,000–40,000 annual income
	Live in urban locations
Usage	Visit the store up to 17 times a year
	Read *Grazia, Hello* and *Vogue* magazines
Attitudes	Like to wear the latest fashions
	Like bargains and are value conscious
	Highly informed about the latest fashions
	Love to shop for exciting products

sector where most brands outsource manufacturing and logistics to partner companies, which slows down the process. Some people may feel that Zara merely copies catwalk designs rather than creating its own, but Zara's customers love the fact that they are able to buy low-cost versions of a design only a few days after it has appeared on the catwalk. Zara is also unusual in that it deliberately restricts the number of each garment it produces and launches around 10,000 new designs each year. This helps customers feel that they have bought something relatively exclusive and ensures that stores always have something new when a customer visits. It has been a winning formula for Zara, which has grown into a huge global brand and business. It now has 1,830 stores in 82 countries with net sales of €8.9 billion in 2012. The success of brands like Zara can be attributed in large part to their use of customer targeting to tailor the brand experience to the customer's needs.

Find underserved customer groups

In any market there are underserved groups of customers. These are distinct from unprofitable ones in that they are currently of low value to the business but have the potential to be converted to high-value, loyal customers. Targeting underserved segments presents new growth opportunities and revenue streams. The ability to identify, attract and meet the needs of such people often goes hand in hand with technological advances. For example, before the invention of the MP3 player people had to choose which cassette or CD they wanted in their car or portable player. Their need was not really "I want just one CD with me" but an unarticulated "I want my music with me when I'm travelling". Technological advances that allowed consumers to easily take their entire music collection with them fulfilled that unarticulated need. Since Apple's iPod was launched in 2001, the market has grown rapidly. Apple's first-year sales of 3.7m had grown to 152m in 2008 and in 2012 it sold 350m iPods.

Net-a-Porter and Mr Porter, high-end online fashion retailers, identified an underserved group of consumers and created a brand and business to serve them. These consumers were wealthy and discerning in their fashion tastes but had little time to spend visiting stores to choose and buy clothes. Mr Porter created an online fashion magazine with advice and clothing co-ordination tips to help customers in their own time online. The clothes are delivered within 24 hours, often to people's work addresses, so that they can take delivery during working hours. Packaged in high-quality materials, with handwritten name tags, the clothes arrive with a luxurious quality that is difficult to convey online. The company's returns policy is also generous, so customers often buy several items, keep the best ones and return the others. Set up in 2000, the company was sold to Richemont, a Swiss luxury goods holding company, for $533m in 2010.

Segmentation methods

Within a single market there will be a range of customer segments, each with its own particular needs, attitudes and values. Marketers can help to identify which products appeal most to each segment and which combinations of product and segment will make the biggest contribution to the business. Through its three car brands, BMW Group targets three different high-value segments. Rolls-Royce is for the super rich, BMW for those who want high performance and status, and Mini for a largely younger, above-average-income group who like the car's performance, size and sense of fun. By using three different brands it is able to make each brand experience distinctive.

Segmentation can be carried out according to:

- demographic information such as age and income;
- usage – the products customers use;
- attitudes – towards a category or socio-cultural issues such as health, ethics, beauty or fashion.

Usually a combination of all three methods helps to provide the most useful description of the segment to target.

Demographic segmentation

Demographic analysis provides a high-level insight into who is buying a product. It gives basic facts about people's life, age, educational level, income and marital status, for example. Companies that can acquire their customers' postcodes can further profile them using secondary data such as that provided by credit-rating agencies. For example, Mosaic, a classification system developed by Experian, a global database company, analyses nationwide trends and demographic data to create 155 person types, aggregated into 67 household types and 15 groups. This creates a three-tier classification to be used at individual, household or postcode level. Although initially developed in the UK, the Mosaic system is now used in some 20 countries around the world, including much of Europe, the United States, East Asia and Australia.

Benefits

Demographic analysis helps identify basic customer types and differences between them. For example, an electricity provider can see which postcodes have a large number of people on higher incomes or families, or both. It might infer that these two customer segments will use more electricity and therefore be of higher value. Armed with this information, the company can adapt its direct marketing campaigns to provide tailored communications and propositions for each of the two household types. Compared with attitudinal segmentation (see below), demographic information is tangible and simple to communicate to the rest of the organisation. It is easy to quantify the average worth of demographic-based segments based on the company's own data or that of secondary providers such as the UK Office of National Statistics, the US FedStats portal or external agencies such as Experian. It is easy to link to other sources of data such as media consumption to create advertising plans.

Weaknesses

Introducing data about the population as a whole rather than a company's specific customers reduces the accuracy of the insights because it does not show whether the people are actually customers of a brand. Demographic information used on its own can invite or encourage stereotyping – that all women aged 20–30 have the same needs or behave in the same way, for example. Furthermore, it can be hard to find meaningful differences between segments using demographics alone. In the case of BMW and Mercedes or Nike and

Adidas, their targets largely have the same demographic profile but very different attitudinal needs.

Usage segmentation

Usage analysis identifies what brands, products or services a group of people actually use, how often they buy them and how much they spend on them. For a mobile phone company, this can be a simple segmentation splitting people into those that pay monthly on a contract and those that "pay as you go" or prepay, topping up their credit with cash as they use the phone. These two segments can be further divided by taking into account the balance of minutes, text message and data or the volume of roaming and international calls. For hotels and airlines, usage segmentation data are often gained through customer loyalty programmes – for example, the number of times and when a guest had stayed at a hotel belonging to the group that year; whether they dined in the restaurant; whether they used the spa; and how much they spent. Usage segmentation also identifies when a product or service is used. For a coffee shop, this might identify a segment that comes in for breakfast before work but not at lunchtime or in the evening.

Benefits

Usage-based segmentations are quick for companies to create and embed because they are based on their own customer data rather than the population as a whole. When linked to customer value, the company can rapidly implement a customer value management approach (see Chapter 1).

Weaknesses

Usage segmentation does not reveal much about the personality of the user. It is of limited help in new product design or for tailoring communication methods and channels. A mobile phone provider's usage data may suggest there are two segments that use a large amount of phone time and texts. But without adding demographic or attitudinal data it is difficult to tell which segment comprises professional workers such as managers and administrators and which manual workers such as plumbers and delivery drivers.

Attitudinal segmentation

Attitudinal data help explain what influences the choices and behaviour of different groups of people. The information provides valuable insight into the personal values and lifestyle of different segments and their enthusiasm (or not) for, say, healthy food or adventurous travel, as well as the image and status a brand may reflect.

Benefits

Attitude-based segmentation gives crucial information about why customers actually buy a brand. It is often used for new product development or developing brand propositions and communication strategies. For example, in the mobile phone products category there may be several distinct attitudinal segments:

- value-conscious and risk-averse consumers who wait till a new technology is fully proven and has come down in price;
- technologically expert consumers who are most interested in the technical and performance features of product;
- status-driven consumers who like to have the latest products but have little interest in the underlying technology.

Each of these segments has demographic and usage differences but also exhibits different attitudes towards technology and buying mobile phones.

Weaknesses

Segmenting by attitude deals with intangible differences that can be hard to pin down. Research rarely identifies singular differences and segments often have overlaps across a range of attitudes. For example, a father might buy cheap bread for his children, healthy bread for himself and luxury bread as a weekend indulgence. It is the same consumer but he is exhibiting several different attitudes to bread buying. Although this makes attitudinal segmentation more insightful and explanatory, it also makes it harder to manage.

Golden rules for segmentation

The segmentation methods used to identify the groups that are the ones it will be most effective to target very much depend on the type of business, the size of its customer base, the resources available and so on. Judgment must also be exercised on how sophisticated any targeting needs to be given the nature of the business and its products. In practice, no single form of segmentation should be used on its own but should form part of a comprehensive picture of the customer.

The golden rules of segmentation are as follows:

1 Start with the customer. Segmenting customers based on variables such as behaviour, attitudes, perceptions, demographics and economic value allows organisations to develop better offerings and targeting strategies. Avoid starting with the company's current products and trying to fit a customer base to these, or simply copying a competitor's target customer.

2 Identify internal audiences and their needs. The research and development (R&D) and new product development (NPD) teams will be most interested in unmet customer needs and ethnographic trends. The customer experience team will want insights from touch point analysis (measuring the satisfaction of relevant contact points from the customer's point of view) and net promoter scores (see Chapter 2) to understand satisfaction drivers. Tactical marketing communications teams, which focus on daily or weekly promotions and discounts, may care more about demographics and media consumption to support the media plan, while those involved in NPD want to know what new features will be required next year.

3 Create meaningful segments. Segments need to be homogeneous in their definition but distinct from each other on needs that are important within a market. Using "importance versus performance" analysis (where the importance of the element of the offer in driving purchase behaviour, or satisfaction, is plotted on the horizontal axis against perception of the firm's performance for that element on the vertical axis) can help to distinguish different segments in a meaningful way. Segments must come across to employees as real and tangible; pen portraits can help make sure that they do. Segment descriptions must include revenue and potential growth expressed not just in volume but also in customer lifetime value (see Chapter 1).

4 Be focused. Segments should be prioritised by how easily the company can serve them and gain the most value. Effective implementation is what matters, rather than targeting everything you can in a half-baked way in a desire for comprehensiveness. However, segmentation evaluations should start by looking at the market as a whole to make sure that new customer types and prospects are not missed.

5 Be pragmatic. Create segments that do not change much over time; the more things get changed, the more the risk of confusion. Segmentation is not an exercise in isolation but a tool to help find and realise the potential of the most valuable customers in a market.

6 Balance current with future. Maximising short-term and long-term profitability requires balancing the needs of current customers with new customers and new needs. Target invested in a multimillion-dollar research programme to identify the changing shopping habits of its customers. The research covered the different life stages that people go through as they get older, such as being single, being a young couple, starting a family, growing older after the children have left home. It found that a typical American consumer would switch to Target after having a baby because the need for bulky non-perishable goods such as nappies combined with tiredness and a lack of time made it a more attractive proposition than a conventional local store. A luxury travel company noticed that its wealthy American customers in their 70s and 80s were quite simply dying out, but the brand's old-fashioned reputation in that market made it unattractive to more youthful retirees and other wealthy customer segments. By commissioning research into other, more youthful segments, the company discovered that younger, wealthy eastern Europeans were as captivated by the brand's old-fashioned British allure as the Americans had been. The strong but literally limited customer lifetime value of the original segment and the new younger segment with far greater future potential became the company's two most profitable customer segments.

Business-to-business segmentation

Segmentation is just as important in business-to-business (B2B) marketing for growth but can be less sophisticated than the best business-to-consumer (B2C) marketing. B2B companies often have a large sales force of account managers whose job is to maintain customer relationships on an individual basis. Each customer might have specific technical needs and this makes it harder to generalise across the business to find segments with common needs. Most B2B companies segment purely on customer size – large corporations versus small and medium-sized enterprises (SMEs) – and within this sometimes by industry sector, such as travel, technology or retail, or by location. But this blunt approach misses several opportunities for both revenue growth and cost reduction. More effective consumer techniques like attitudes towards the product category and targeting can unlock new growth opportunities even in B2B companies.

Managing stakeholders

A 2011 worldwide survey conducted by Havas Media found that nearly 85% of consumers expect companies to become actively involved in promoting individual and collective well-being, but only 28% think companies are working hard enough to solve the big social and environmental challenges. Companies must remember that customers are not the only stakeholders to target. The range and number of stakeholders that can have an impact on a company's business are growing and this means managers need to have a good understanding of each stakeholder group's needs and potential influence. Stakeholder mapping helps with this (see Figure 4.2).

The marketing actions that can be taken to engage different stakeholder groups are covered in detail in Chapter 9, but the following example shows how effective stakeholder management can help a business grow. Chipotle, an American burrito restaurant chain founded in 1993, has identified four stakeholder groups (beyond its customers) with specific needs that affect its business's performance.

FIG 4.2 **A typical stakeholder map**

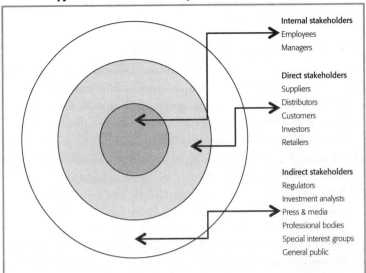

Internal stakeholders
Employees
Managers

Direct stakeholders
Suppliers
Distributors
Customers
Investors
Retailers

Indirect stakeholders
Regulators
Investment analysts
Press & media
Professional bodies
Special interest groups
General public

Chipotle's strategy is to sell "Food with Integrity" and its main product is good value burritos. This means using only naturally reared or grown foods, looking after employees' welfare, trying to source ingredients locally to reduce environmental waste and not using harmful cooking oil. Many of its buildings have recycling facilities and are energy efficient. Its consumer target is 18–34 year olds with a college degree and an above-average income. Compared with other fast-food brands, Chipotle manages to balance this consumer segment's needs for good-value, filling food with the desire to eat more healthily. While consumers are its primary stakeholders, there are four other important stakeholder groups to manage.

■ **Employees.** Because integrity is a central part of the brand proposition this helps guide the way that the company treats and manages its employees. For example, it has an English-language learning programme that helps its diverse set of employees improve their communications skills as well as clear policies against worker exploitation.

- **Suppliers.** Chipotle attempts to source its ingredients from local and organic farms where possible by building strong relationships with local farmers. It also encourages the rearing of naturally raised livestock such as cows, chickens and pigs.

- **Government.** There are a large number of food, health and safety regulations that restaurants must comply with. Chipotle's desire to deliver food with integrity led its founder, Steve Ells, to address the American Congress in 2009 to try to eliminate the use of antibiotics in livestock rearing.

- **Investors.** In order to grow rapidly, Chipotle carefully managed its relationships with investors. One of them, McDonald's, a fast-food restaurant, invested over $360m in Chipotle between 2001 and 2006 in exchange for shares, eventually making it the company's majority shareholder. This new cash and McDonald's expertise helped Chipotle grow from under 20 restaurants to over 500 in just a few years before its initial public offering (IPO) in 2006.

The combination of a clear target audience with its great food offer, powerful brand proposition and careful management of its various stakeholders has worked well. When Chipotle launched on the New York Stock Exchange (NYSE) in 2006 its share price doubled from $22 to $44 in just one day making it the highest rising IPO share on the NYSE in the previous five years. It now has 1,458 restaurants across the United States, Canada and the UK, with revenues of $2.2 billion and a gross profit of $215m in 2011.

Partnerships

Most companies rely on others to help deliver the total customer experience. Haier is the world's largest white-goods manufacturer with an 8.6% global market share in 2012. It relies on thousands of other businesses – from materials and motor suppliers, to logistics and delivery partners – to help it get it fridges and freezers to consumers all over the world. Managing these relationships is crucial to its continued success. Many companies rank their suppliers and other partners on their level of importance to the business, with those in tier one being critical to the immediate and overall business performance and those in tier three being less important. Managers invest significant time and energy in nurturing these relationships so that they remain strong, productive and reliable.

A well-chosen brand as a partner can increase preference and advocacy for the master brand. In 2009 Holiday Inn, a hotel chain, switched from serving its own coffee in conference meeting rooms to getting Starbucks to provide it, which resulted in improved customer perceptions of the Holiday Inn brand. Its brand promise as the best place to stay or have business meetings was enhanced by working with a strong brand with better credentials in the hot drinks category. Managers need to decide which type of partnership – explicit and branded like the Starbucks example or hidden and unbranded – will deliver the maximum financial benefit. There are many different types of partnership that range in complexity from a standard supplier contract to outsourcing service delivery through to a fully co-branded service proposition (see Figure 4.3). The choice of partnership and overt branding depends on how strong the company brand is in a specific customer segment compared with the potential partner brand. Such partnerships are becoming more common as brands seek additional competitive advantage, as Holiday Inn achieved.

Businesses seeking rapid and/or extensive geographical growth seek appropriate partnerships to help them. This is especially true where growth requires more investment – financial or resources – than a single brand is able to muster. Chipotle's partnership with McDonald's is a good example.

FIG 4.3 **Brand partnership types**

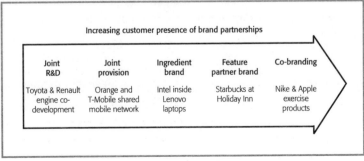

The role of partner brands

Many service businesses use intermediaries for distribution. Airlines sell tickets through travel agents and online companies such as Expedia and Travelocity as well as through their own channels. Insurance brands such as Axa, Allianz and Zurich sell through high-street banks as well as their own agents and brokers. Mobile phone network brands such as Vodafone, T-Mobile and AT&T sell contracts through their own stores as well as independent ones such as Best Buy in the United States and Carphone Warehouse (The Phone House) in Europe. The economics of increased reach far outweigh the direct revenues lost to third parties and lower margins from using the resale model. Intermediaries are adding value and therefore profitability for themselves through their ability to focus on their service offer and they may provide better service than the original network operators.

Managing large groups of third-party agents or intermediaries presents a significant challenge to marketers to maintain consistency of customer experience without full control of that experience. Mostly partner brands will be acting on behalf of the master brand. For example, a master brand such as Vodafone will be the primary brand that a mobile phone customer has a relationship with because it is fulfilling the contract, while the Best Buy or Carphone Warehouse brands may take the minor role of selling the contract in the first place. However, customers often view the seller as the primary brand in the relationship. If a flight is delayed, customers may first blame the airline brand rather than the airport authority that may have caused it. The key to creating value for both partner brands is to clearly signal the role that each plays in the service delivery. Often this comes down to specifically labelling or highlighting the contribution at that moment in the customer journey. For example:

- "Intel inside" demonstrates the ingredient brand role that Intel semiconductor chips play with many computer brands;
- One World or Star Alliance airline networks highlight partner airlines that have connecting routes and shared loyalty schemes;
- "Search by Google" indicates that the powerful search engine is behind the service offered by a much smaller, branded website.

Regulators

External regulatory stakeholders may affect a business's ability to operate. Businesses in sensitive areas such as pharmaceuticals, banking and defence require stringent regulatory checks and licences. Other businesses such as food retailing and car manufacturing have to comply with, for example, health and safety regulations, and they need to work with regulators to make sure that they meet the appropriate standards. This requires delicate reputation management by companies so that regulators perceive them as trustworthy and capable.

Special interest groups

There are other stakeholders that indirectly affect a business, particularly customers' and employees' perceptions of the brand. The power of special interest groups has increased significantly with the growth of social media, allowing individuals to share their views with potentially millions of others. Pressure groups fighting for human rights have accused big, global brands like Apple, Adidas and Nike of allowing poor conditions for workers in their factories. And Greenpeace, an environmental organisation, continues to campaign against large energy brands like Shell, BP and Exxon and their drilling operations around the world.

A stakeholder map should identify such special interest groups so that policy, plans and management resources can be allocated to make sure that their needs are accommodated. Quantitative research helps develop a profile of each stakeholder group's brand perceptions and influence on other stakeholder groups on the map and the business itself. Annual surveys can then build up a picture of how well the company is managing its various stakeholders over time.

Summary

Targeting is one of the most useful ways to achieve more profitable growth and improve customer lifetime value. It ensures that company resources are invested where they will achieve higher returns. There are many approaches to defining customer targets or segments and companies should avoid using a single segmentation technique in isolation. Combining different approaches such as demographic, usage and attitudinal segmentation to achieve a specific business objective increases the likelihood of success. Crucially, it opens the way to the achievement of maximum cost effectiveness and optimal growth tailored for customer needs and the market.

5 Market opportunities for growth

EVERY BUSINESS NEEDS to keep an eye on opportunities for it to grow, using the research that marketers can undertake into market penetration, market expansion, product development and diversification.

Market penetration

Getting existing customers of a product to purchase more of your brand's product, and thereby increasing market share, is one way for a business to grow. Apple is one company that has been extraordinarily successful in inspiring an emotional commitment to the brand through customer relevance, competitive differentiation and company authenticity, so much so that its customers are unusually loyal and many own several different Apple products. (Relevance, differentiation and authenticity are the building blocks of a brand proposition and are explored in more detail in Chapter 6.)

It is only possible to increase market penetration with a product that many consumers can easily consume more of. The total market for luxury cars like Rolls-Royce is limited and therefore offers limited potential for further market penetration by that brand. Alternatively, a business can increase its market penetration in a wider sense if it has a portfolio of products that can be more effectively cross-sold to customers. In both cases, it involves targeting a customer base that is known to like the brand and is therefore the lowest-risk, lowest-cost option in pursuing growth.

Price considerations

One of the keys to selling more of the same product to existing customers is to make them less likely to switch to another brand. To make sure that a customer buys a company's product rather than another brand, it must be attractive enough for the customer to choose it even when there is price or promotional competition from the other brand. As Larry Light, chief brand officer at InterContinental Hotels Group and former CMO at McDonald's, stated:

> You can't have enduring growth of the bottom line unless you have quality growth of the top line. When I started at McDonald's, the vast majority of all advertising and promotion spend was on "Deal of the month" and three years later it was less than 20% and the stock price had gone from $13 to $68 per share.

McDonald's had increased the value it delivered to its customers and reduced its reliance on price promotions to keep customers buying at full price.

Price promotions may boost short-term sales as switchers rush to stock up on low-price goods. But this simply encourages price seeking rather than brand loyalty. Insurance aggregator sites that search the cheapest options for, say, car insurance perform the same function: they reduce the market to one that is price rather than value driven. The use of product bundles that are attractively priced but marketed as much if not more on their other benefits is a more effective way to generate repeat purchasing. Bundling a group of same-brand products is another way of increasing sales of a product while avoiding a direct price war. Retail promotions offering "3 for the price of 2" of a branded product create a highly attractive cost-benefit equation, encouraging customers to purchase more products without directly dropping the official unit price of the product. This works as a temporary measure, but if these types of discount are offered too frequently, consumers will begin to perceive the product as worth less than the official unit price.

More uses, more sales

It is difficult to persuade customers to buy more of a product when they cannot see that they have a use for it. But if you can show them alternative uses or occasions when it might be useful, this can create a more sustainable increase in sales than that which results from pure price promotion. Customers are more likely to remain loyal to a brand if it offers something extra. Exploring how a product or service might be more useful or appealing is an essential stage in the process of increasing purchase frequency and loyalty. McDonald's restaurants were typically used just for breakfast, lunch and dinner, and so the company decided to create other occasions or reasons to visit the restaurant to drive additional sales. By offering higher-quality and more varieties of coffee and greater pastry choices, McDonald's was able to encourage its customers to make more use of, and spend more in, its restaurants through additional visits. The changes also attracted new customers. Similarly, Procter & Gamble has persuaded existing and new customers that Flash is not just a floor cleaner but also good for all types of kitchen and bathroom surface cleaning.

Getting messages across about the benefits of a brand that are not normally associated with it carries a cost and risks alienating customers if the message is hard to believe. The new benefit or use must be perceived as real and genuinely useful rather than a gimmick. Well-known as a low-cost leisure airline, easyJet wanted to increase the number of business travellers who used it. To do so it had to convince them to switch from traditional, full-service airlines to easyJet. Flexible fares, communicated through an advertising campaign, were specifically designed to appeal to business travellers, according to Carolyn McCall, CEO of easyJet. Examples included "Flexible fares from £79 pounds, that's business sense", offering customers the additional benefit of flexible flight times while retaining cheap prices. Revenues rose by 9.2% in the first quarter of 2013, which the company claimed was partly a result of an increase in business travellers, who were also trying to save money.

Cross-selling and upselling

When a company has a portfolio of products, marketers should look for links that might help persuade customers of one product to buy others. This might be through promotions and new uses or benefits, as described above, or it may be through bundling, where there is no need to involve third parties. For example, the Ariel clothes-washing powder and Lenor fabric softener brands are both owned by Procter & Gamble and could be used together in an effective consumer promotion.

Cross-selling involves getting customers to buy additional products alongside their primary purchase. This is most effective when these are naturally accompanying products rather than random additions. For cross-selling to work it must make sense to the person who is targeted; just because a firm sells soap and soup does not mean that it can successfully cross-sell soup to soap customers or vice versa. Attempting to do so could simply put customers off. Furthermore, making people aware of the spread of a business's brands and products can be counterproductive if they jar with their interests and emotions. For example, white-goods manufacturers often try to cross-sell extended warranties when a customer buys a new washing machine or fridge. The product may have a standard one-year warranty, but the extended version may cover the first three years of the product's life. A camera retailer might recommend that a customer buying a camera should buy an additional lens, a camera case or battery packs. Because these additions make sense and improve the total experience of the camera, they are likely to result in cross-sales.

Upselling involves getting a customer to purchase a more expensive version of the product they originally wanted. This is usually based on emphasising the product's better performance or higher quality. Businesses need to design their product ranges in increments that make sense to the customer. If they do not, it is less likely that customers will upgrade. For example, customers might well upgrade from a 40-inch to a 42-inch or 50-inch television because the increase in size and the difference in price are small, but if the only options are 20-inch or 50-inch the chance of them upgrading will be minimal. Similarly, a customer may want to buy the budget version of a washing machine, but the product and performance differences may convince them to buy a more expensive and higher specification machine. Such upselling succeeds because the improved benefits of the higher-priced options are clearly identified.

Market expansion

By expanding the reach of their distribution and marketing, businesses can sell their products to new customers in new markets. Red Bull, an energy-drinks company, grew dramatically by expanding geographically yet targeting a similar youth audience in each market. Events such as the Red Bull Flugtag, an air show held in a different country every year in which homemade aircraft are launched from a pier, were designed to appeal to a demographic group rather than a nationality. The company's sponsorship of Felix Baumgartner's record-breaking parachute jump from the edge of space in 2012 may have been a significant news event worldwide, but it is the brand's local activity in its various markets that cements its reputation with its target audience, and as it has grown it has been able to transfer what it has learnt to new markets. There is now a tried and tested model for introducing the product into new markets with the right cultural and demographic fit. Where a new market has, through research, been identified as fertile ground for a product, it provides a medium-risk, medium-cost opportunity for growth. More difficult, when many new markets offer potential for growth, is deciding where limited resources should be invested.

During the 1990s, marketing strategies emphasised a globally consistent brand approach and message, but more recently there has been a shift towards localised strategies. InterContinental Hotels Group (IHG), for example, launched a health and fitness oriented mid-market hotel brand called Even in the United States in 2012. Even Hotels offer special health food and drink options, free filtered drinking water and best-in-class gyms for individuals and group exercise activities. This helps demonstrate increased relevance for American travellers but also differentiates it from other hotel chains. IHG also launched an upmarket Asian hotel brand Hualuxe initially focusing on China in 2012. As well as offering Chinese food and drink with noodle bars and traditional tea shops, emphasis is given to making a show of the arrivals process and providing "hosts" to help guests during their stay. Again, this helps demonstrate relevance for Chinese customers while differentiating from other international hotel brands in China. The decision to develop distinct brands for different markets signals a shift from the traditional global "one size fits all" brand strategy of previous decades. The difference is that it is helping to expand the markets for fitness-conscious travellers and travellers in China by offering distinct and dedicated services rather than using globally recognised homogeneous products. IHG seeks to maximise returns in its two large and most important travel markets, the United States and China, rather than spread its investment too thinly across the 100 countries in which it operates. Both of these sub-brands have been created to maximise their share of the growing fitness and Chinese luxury travel markets. If the strategy works, IHG will no doubt introduce sub-brands in other countries too – if it sees a clear market growth opportunity.

It is the role of the board to set an overall growth framework in terms of targets and risk for the managers of the business to make their decisions about how to pursue growth. Marketers can play a significant role in setting the growth agenda as they have direct access to customer and competitor information. They can use these insights to help manage the marketing budget to maximise effectiveness. It helps if they see themselves as portfolio asset managers, whose role – similar to that of investment portfolio managers in the financial sector – is to balance levels of risk and reward to maximise overall global marketing performance. It is a role that requires the understanding and knowledge of, and sensitivity to, each market, and this can only be gained from robust data and qualitative local feedback.

Marketers can analyse the mix of growth markets. The current value to the business and the potential returns of each have to be assessed, which involves looking at such matters as market share, competitive barriers, product maturity within a market and the overall market maturity. From this analysis it becomes easier to make decisions about how to invest across markets that involve different levels of risk to help achieve the overall company growth target.

ING Direct, a Dutch bank that operates in around 40 countries, has in recent years focused its growth strategy on just eight markets – Austria, Canada, France, Germany, Italy, Spain, the UK and the United States – which, because of the high number of consumers happy to bank online, were well suited to its business model. Marketing investment therefore mirrored the growth opportunities in these countries while providing only "maintenance" investment in the other 32 markets. In the United States, the bank's "Your number" advertising campaign, with its friendly approach and use of non-technical language, was particularly successful in attracting new customers. It featured real customers, each of whom had a precise target for their pension pot. ING used this approach in other growth markets, making the brand consistent and reducing marketing costs.

In a large company operating in many markets, portfolio asset management requires a clear understanding of a company's categories of products (asset classes for investors) and a good sense of their potential in different markets. The range of products might include risky and nascent ones as well as more mature and stable ones. Toyota, a Japanese carmaker, invested heavily in hybrid technology cars such as the Prius, which is selling well in the West, while it carries on selling huge numbers of its low-cost Swift model in emerging markets such as India and Brazil. When managing a portfolio of brand assets, markets should be classified as one of the following: core, high growth, strategically important.

Core markets

It is typical for global companies to have between seven and ten markets that account for the bulk of their revenues and therefore drive most investment decisions. These usually include their home market and any market where they have a stockmarket listing.

High-growth markets

These depend on the sector and category and the level of market maturity. High growth traditionally refers to markets that have a compound annual growth rate (CAGR) of at least 10%. The CAGR is the combined rate of growth, typically over the past 2–3 years. For example, if a market grows from $100m to $150m (+50%) in year one and shrinks by $50m to $100m (–33%) in year two, the CAGR is 0% as the market has not grown at all over the two years.

The CAGR enables more accurate projections to be made to inform investment decisions. For some emerging markets it can reach 40%, while for mature markets it may even be negative. High-growth markets offer high rewards for those that accept the higher risks and are agile enough to make the most of the market dynamics.

Strategically important markets

Markets can be strategically important for a variety of reasons:

- **Home market.** The market that a company is based in has additional strategic implications for legal, tax, employee and investor relations. While many Western companies may not be deriving much growth or profits from their home market, it is unthinkable that Vodafone would abandon the UK market or Citroën the French market, even if those markets account for only a small proportion of their global sales and profits. The home market is where the company's board members usually reside, and is often the location of its primary stock-exchange listing and main share-price analysts. Thus business performance and issues in the home market have a significant effect on the perceptions and share price of the company.

- **Product markets.** Many companies manufacture their products in low-cost markets even if they sell little there. They can be significant employers in those markets, so maintaining good employee relations and factory conditions are critical to their success. Some global fashion brands have suffered following reports of poor employee conditions or fires at their factories. Consequently, many brands, including Walmart, Gap and Primark, have improved labour and factory conditions, even though this affects profits. They know that poor publicity will cost more than any improvements.

- **Global reach.** For a company to claim global reach, it may be necessary to establish a presence in some countries through perhaps little more than a marketing and sales office. Banks, for instance, often serve countries that reflect the location of their global customers even if the geographic collection seems unusual. These markets are maintained but they are not expected to produce returns that significantly affect overall company performance.

■ **Emerging markets.** As the name suggests, these are markets that seem to offer the prize of future potential growth. For example, L'Oréal, a French cosmetics company, has experienced a dramatic increase in sales in India and is targeting $1.3 billion sales there by 2020, more than five times expected sales in 2012. Companies try to identify the most attractive new growth markets and invest in them before they are fully developed, knowing that it may take a number of years to get sizeable returns. They balance this increased risk with increased expected returns.

Product development

If a business extends its product range, it can capitalise on existing brand awareness and loyalty. Product development is considered a low-risk path to growth if a business is selling to an existing, loyal customer base, though initial development costs may be high. Unilever's Dove skincare range began with a moisturising bath product that cleansed and helped with dry and damaged skin. The core proposition was that Dove was both gentle and convenient, a standpoint from which other skincare and personal hygiene products – such as deodorants and shampoos – could be developed and marketed.

Dove's subsequent expansion into the men's skincare market did not fit with its existing target market. However, Unilever, which owns the Axe (Lynx in the UK) range of deodorants and shower gels, was aware that teenage users of the Axe brand had no Unilever brand to graduate to so they moved on to Nivea or L'Oréal – hence the decision to launch Dove Men+Care in 2010. As a general rule, product and brand extensions should not diverge far from the core proposition, but diversification (see below) is an alternative route to growth.

The advantage of being fast and first

Businesses, like athletes, succeed by getting ahead and staying ahead of their competitors. Being first to market gives many firms a long-term advantage, and an ability to stay at the forefront of consumer preference makes all the difference between success and failure. Being quick to spot and respond to market opportunities – to hit the moment when the consumer appetite is ripe – is a characteristic of many highly successful businesses, as is their ability to improve and differentiate and add value to a new product when faced with a competitive threat.

The Sony Walkman transformed the way people listened to recorded music and for years its dominant position in the portable music category seemed unassailable. But then came the game-changing MP3 player, a 1994 invention of Karlheinz Brandenburg. A few South Korean companies including SaeHan/Eiger, Cowon and Diamond Rio tried to reach the mass market with the new the product and format, and had some success. Then on October 23rd 2001 Apple launched its first 5-gigabyte iPod, which quickly came to dominate the music player market. Despite being a follower rather than the first to market, it transformed portable music listening in the eyes of consumers. Apple has sold more than 300m iPods. Diamond Rio, by contrast, stopped making MP3 players in 2005. Apple's genius was not in creating a category-transforming technology, but in its insight and understanding of what consumers wanted and in providing that with technical excellence and design panache. Apple's faster, more expansive and more innovative development programme gave it further edge over the competition and helped consolidate its market dominance. It is a model of how rapid prototyping techniques can be used to build market dominance.

Google is another firm that tries to dominate markets through quick development of its products. Its famous line "always in Beta" means just that: the company would rather get products out to the market quickly and evolve them than wait until they are extensively tested and refined before launching them. This gives it a significant advantage over competitors that wait until their products are fully tested and refined. Google instead encourages users to provide feedback and help fine tune the product once it is in the marketplace. It is a process based on the idea of continuous improvement and the idea that nothing can ever at any time be perfect. Of course, software has often been sold on this basis but it is increasingly being used for other products. Google ran a competition for consumers to apply for an early version of its new head-up-display device, Google Glass. Applicants had to state why they believed they should be given this product and be willing to pay $1,000 for the privilege. Those selected provided feedback quickly and on a scale that would normally have taken many years to obtain. This means that Google can release an updated product much faster than it could using traditional techniques and make sure that there is a closer fit to consumer needs. For marketing teams, this means greater openness to involving consumers in the design and development of products and services. These small "test and learn" pilot programmes can benefit businesses by rapidly improving propositions on a small scale before expanding.

Product life cycles

Every product has a life cycle that needs to be understood to maximise financial returns. A new market may emerge for lithium-battery-powered cars. At first, only a few customers may be willing to try them. But as the technology improves and the price comes down the market grows, until, for example, it is superseded by another technology like that of Honda's hydrogen-powered FCX Clarity car.

The product life cycle of a new smartphone with a bigger screen may begin with a few early adopters who are willing to try something new, probably at a higher price. As the product becomes more accepted, more people buy it, creating more sales for the brand. This helps lower the costs of production, encouraging more people to buy. There is a period when there are lots of people buying the product with little investment by the company. But as the smartphone is superseded by one with an even bigger screen or better features, sales start to decrease.

The introduction of new product models needs to be managed to maximise the yield from each model or version. Quite modest enhancements can significantly extend a product's life without the need for an expensive and extensive revamp. A product's expected life cycle and its expected financial return over the cycle are essential components of the investment case that is made for it. Figure 5.1 illustrates a typical product life cycle, known as a bell curve: the rise to maturity and the decline thereafter. Among the challenges for marketers are to speed up the trial period so as to get the product established in the market as early as possible, and to extend the maturity phase before decline.

FIG 5.1 **The product life cycle**

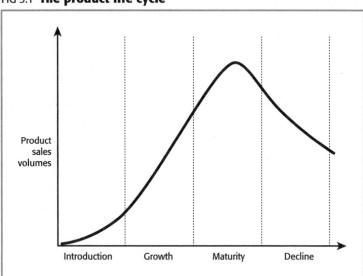

Product
sales
volumes

Introduction   Growth   Maturity   Decline

In practice, most products are imitated, losing their competitive advantage over time. This is most obvious in fast-moving consumer goods (FMCG) such as washing powder, food and skincare. Procter & Gamble launched a new Tide washing powder with a two-ingredient formula. This created an initial differentiation and a fresh price premium within the category, but as other firms introduced competing products with similar benefits of cleaning agent and stain remover the advantage was cut, and to stay ahead of the competition Procter & Gamble launched another new Tide washing product called "Pods", this time based on a unique three-ingredient formula that cleans, fights stains and brightens clothes. The aim for firms operating in sectors such as FMCG should be to pursue a product innovation strategy that combines incremental change with the occasional seismic leap.

Platform-driven growth

The Gillette razor range is a well-known example of how cleverly an innovation strategy of the kind touched on above can be pursued in what is known as platform-driven growth. Substantial investment is made in a core "platform", often a main product component or technology, which can then be adapted and enhanced at relatively low cost. Customers who have bought into the platform are kept intrigued and satisfied by the enhancements made, while the high initial investment in the platform can be amortised over the extended life the incremental improvements enable the product to enjoy. It is a strategy that is used for both high-cost and low-cost goods. Volkswagen Audi Group (VAG) produces numerous different car models that use the same underlying platform but are sold with four different brand names: Seat, Skoda, Volkswagen and Audi. The mechanics and the chassis are similar (the 1.2 litre TSi engine is used in all four brands) and these are adapted with different consumer interiors and exteriors to emphasise a different brand experience for a different target audience.

The financial benefit of these platform-based manufacturing systems is enormous. What has to be watched is the risk of creating two products so similar that they simply take market share from each other; when low-margin products cannibalise the sales of high-margin products it means less profit for the overall business.

Platform-based growth depends on being clear about the benefits consumers will pay extra for and those they would prefer to do without in return for a cost saving. Price sensitivity models can be used to show how much more money a brand can charge for a differentiated and relevant experience, and other financial models will help determine which product option will generate the biggest overall return. (See also Chapter 7 on brand portfolio growth, which looks in more depth at brand extension strategies.)

Diversification

Another way for a business to grow is by diversifying into new products or services, which may be done organically or via acquisition of another business. Sometimes firms pursue a strategy of vertical integration – that is, involving themselves in stages further up or down the supply/value chain, for example not only making products but also selling them through retail outlets. Apple does this with its computers and other technology products, controlling their manufacture and selling them through its own stores and online (as well as through other retailers at unvarying prices). This helps to make sure that it is not possible to buy its products at discounted prices, thus maintaining its prestige and reinforcing the incentive to buy directly from Apple. In short, Apple does all it can to control or "own" the customer relationship through its sales and distribution arrangements and to extract value from the supply chain at every stage.

Virgin Atlantic has focused on the other end of the supply chain by investing in a biofuel refinery in California, thus giving the company greater control over the supply and price of the fuel it needs for its fleet of aircraft. Having more control of this high variable cost makes good commercial sense.

Having a strong brand proposition makes it easier to sell unrelated products under a single brand because the brand reassures customers that the organisation is a credible supplier of these products. This is why large supermarket chains like Carrefour, Walmart and Tesco have diversified their businesses horizontally by moving into non-food areas such as clothing, mobile phones, insurance and banking services. However, horizontal diversification can be risky: it is likely to be costly if new products are developed from scratch or are acquired through the purchase of another business, and a high level of marketing skill may be required to win customers over to the diversification. The risk can be reduced by – as many supermarket groups do – sourcing goods in from experienced producers and selling them under the retailer's own brand – a practice referred to as "white labelling".

Breaking the mould

Transformation of a product category has been responsible for the rapid rise and decline of some of the world's biggest brands over the past few decades. In the mobile phone industry, the top two brands by market share have changed from Nokia and Motorola to Samsung and Apple. With the creation of smartphones, these two brands have transformed the category from standard talk and text phones to powerful hand-held computers. Nokia and Motorola failed to understand how much customers would value mobile internet-based services such as Facebook, Gmail and GPS mapping tools above traditional talking and texting. This evolution in consumer mobile phone usage has had a dramatic impact on shareholder value. According to Thomson Reuters analysis carried out in 2011, earnings per share (EPS) for Nokia was 73% lower in 2011 than it had been in 2006, whereas Apple's EPS had risen by 65% over the same period. Yet Nokia had a dominant share of 35% of the worldwide mobile phone market in 2006, the year before Apple launched its first iPhone. By 2012, Apple's market share had grown from zero to 5% while Nokia's had dropped to 23.6%. This turnaround in fortunes of the two brands emphasises the difference it can make if you succeed in redefining a product category. Nokia is not alone; Kodak is another notable brand that failed to appreciate that its traditional category (camera film) was being redefined almost out of existence.

Spanx, a brand of women's "elasticated slimming underwear", which came to the market in 2000, is a classic case of how customer insight can lead to a category being redefined. Started by Sarah Blakely, Spanx now has an annual turnover of $250m and net margins of around 20%, and Blakely became the youngest ever self-made billionaire in the 2012 *Forbes* list of billionaires. Because of her own experience of uncomfortable undergarments, Blakely set about reinventing women's girdles with new materials and designs. Spanx not only transformed a product but also created a fresh category of products. Although it has spawned a series of competitor products, it continues to be the category leader by some margin.

A strategy focused on category transformation is bold and risky, involving a high level of investment, but first-movers can make huge returns. YouTube was one of the early social-media sites that encouraged consumers to become amateur film directors. Its success was based on rapid peaks of excitement that surrounded the most unlikely video clips. Viral interest in these videos often swept around the world in a matter of days, garnering hundreds of millions of advocates. It is the kind of word-of-mouth promotion that consumer brands can only dream of. YouTube, which has made improbable stars of members of the public who post funny videos, was sold to Google just 18 months after it was formed in February 2005 for $1.65 billion and it has continued to grow rapidly, with gross revenues of nearly $1.7 billion in 2012. Contrast this with Bebo, a social-media site aimed at teenagers. Launched also in 2005 it initially grew rapidly and was sold in 2008 to AOL for $850m. However, its popularity waned just as rapidly and in 2010 AOL sold it to a venture capital firm, Criterion Capital Partners, for just $10m. It had lost 99% of its value in just two years. And then in 2013 it was bought by its original creator for $1m.

Elon Musk, one of the founders of PayPal, a leading online payments system, has continued his category-busting approach with the launch of Tesla Motors. He has described his vision to create an electric car that is fast and sexy and thus gives the lie to the supposed truths that sports cars are not green and that green cars are slow and unglamorous as follows: "Our goal has always been to build the best car in the world and set new standards for safety, driving range, design and performance." Tesla's latest Model S car accelerates from 0 to 100 kilometres per hour in 4.4 seconds, faster than an Aston Martin DB9 and at less than half the price.

FIG 5.2 **Category transformation matrix: washing powders**

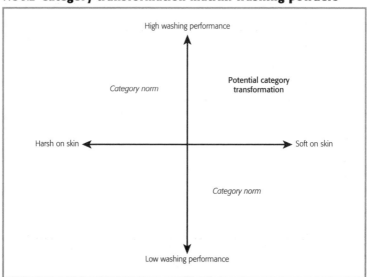

Source: www.senate.eu.com

Marketers can use the matrix in Figure 5.2 in any category to establish the category norms then search for category-shifting opportunities. These can be at a category level such as electric versus petrol cars or at a category differentiation level such as new washing powders that offer high performance and are soft on hands and clothes.

Opportunity assessment

The four main types of market-led growth – market penetration, market development, product development and diversification – have been described above. But to decide which is the best strategy to follow a business must determine the most attractive market/product/ customer combinations that it can serve better and at lower cost than anyone else. It can do this by assessing how competitive its products are in a market or category. In the early 1970s McKinsey and General Electric (GE) created a 3 × 3 matrix to help assess GE's portfolio of products and identify the strongest combinations of product category and market growth opportunity (see Figure 5.3).

FIG 5.3 **McKinsey and GE opportunity matrix**

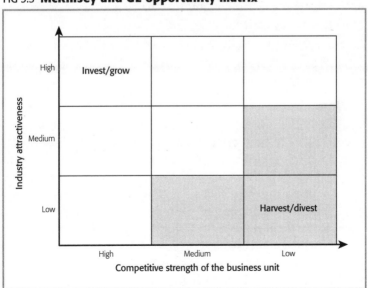

Sources: GE; McKinsey & Company

Clearly those with a higher sustainable competitive advantage in highly attractive categories are the most important to pursue. Equally, those products with generic benefits in shrinking categories should be shut down or sold. Looking at the market opportunities for growth also provides an opportunity to do some spring-cleaning.

Potential value assessment

When seeking to identify the revenue growth that a new business might bring, marketers will typically examine specific customer segments, product ranges or markets to get as clear and accurate a picture as possible. Data from quantitative research helps to test a new proposal in advance of launching it with real customers. Historic analysis using regression techniques (see Chapter 2) can provide a useful benchmark for comparing various new opportunities or for comparing current performance against the new venture. Revenue growth predictions can be split into three components:

■ **Volume.** How big is the new market opportunity? How many customers will buy the new product?

■ **Value.** How much is it worth? How much more are customers willing to pay for the new product?

■ **Probability.** How likely is it to happen? How realistic is it that customers will change their behaviour and buy the new product rather than the old one?

For example, a mobile phone company might use this method to quantify the revenue growth opportunity from a new, targeted customer-service strategy. It also provides the management team with an estimate of the "at risk" revenues they might lose should the standard of service disappoint customers. Estimates are made of the volume of current customers in segment A who might switch away from the brand, and of the volume of the total market of segment A who might switch to using the brand. The revenue value of the potential new customers in segment A is then calculated using data about the average current spend or average revenue per user (ARPU). And, finally, the probability of people switching either way is calculated by using an average percentage of the past three years of switching behaviour for segment A. Typically, a range of high and low probabilities is used to create a range value. In simple numbers, the revenue opportunity calculation might look like that in Table 5.1.

TABLE 5.1 **Opportunity assessment for a mobile phone company**

	Low estimate	High estimate
Volume of current segment A with media brand	350,000	350,000
Volume of segment A in total market segment	2m	2m
Net volume opportunity for new customers	115,500	165,000
Value of current ARPU for the mobile brand for segment A	$900 per year	$900 per year
Probability of switching away from the mobile brand	7% 24,500	10% 35,000
Probability of switching to the mobile brand	7% 140,000	10% 200,000
Total revenue opportunity	$103.95m	$148.50m

Most chief executives will favour investment only if the low estimate generates an acceptable return for the business. They prudently assume that there will be unforeseen internal costs and delays combined with potential external factors, such as competitors reducing their prices, which might make the low estimate all the more likely to be the actual outcome.

Costing a new service venture or product range

The other half of the calculation is to understand the likely costs of achieving any revenue growth. This means calculating what it will take to please (or "delight" in marketing jargon) and therefore retain current customers and get new customers to try a new service or product range. Delighted customers are more likely to be strong advocates for the brand with higher than average spend and profitability. Costs are easier to estimate and less subject to variation than revenues, particularly if the new venture is based on a product or service that exists already. There are two types of costs involved in a new venture:

- costs in developing the new venture – investment and development costs for R&D and capital expenditure on equipment and materials (capex);
- costs when operating the new venture – operating costs for staff, stock and services.

Investment costs include those needed to create and develop the new product or service, such as R&D, patent registration, market testing and piloting. Capital expenditure might include machinery, websites, call centres, store refits, or additional buildings. Investment costs need to be recovered over the life of the new product and are typically amortised or depreciated over the first 1–3 years of a product's life. The operating costs required to deliver the product or service year after year include costs such as manufacturing, sales, marketing and distribution.

It is better to overestimate rather than underestimate development costs to reduce the risk of failing as a result of underinvestment. One way of doing this is to include an overall contingency percentage, which makes the process more transparent. Cost overruns tend to be remembered even when the outcome has been successful; cost savings rarely are. Lastly, there is always an intangible "cost of change" factor, which may mean that an organisation (especially if it is a large one) favours a couple of big projects rather than many small ones. If the initial cost and projected return of a new investment is not substantial, the board may say "why bother?".

Balancing costs with likely sales volumes allows strategic choices to be made about product positioning and its evolution over time. The choice may be to enter with a low-cost, high-demand product or with a high-cost niche product. The following chapter explores the concept of the brand proposition, which is fundamental in determining such matters.

Focused investment

Not all market opportunities are equally important. Focusing on the most promising ones and generating higher returns is where the marketing effort of a business is best applied. This may mean that there have to be difficult conversations with colleagues responsible for different markets and products. It certainly argues for transparency in planning and decision-making and the dissemination of marketing knowledge, skills and practice around the organisation. The marketing actions required for low-growth and high-growth opportunities are different. For example, mature markets are often saturated, so the task of marketing is to build differentiation and loyalty in order to retain current customers and increase cross-selling of more products to them. High-growth markets require market education to explain the relevance of a new product to new customers and to encourage them to try it.

In the past, the accepted wisdom was that global brands needed global propositions and marketing campaigns. This can be true if the product or service offers a benefit that is universally compelling, but with many brands, products and services it is different benefits that resonate with different individuals in different countries. Vodafone, a mobile phone network, uses a global–local approach to marketing. While most countries use the Vodafone master brand and identity, many of the products and services, such as the loyalty scheme and technical support propositions, are tailored in individual markets (see Table 5.2). This ensures that each market is able to optimise its own-brand marketing.

TABLE 5.2 **Vodafone's local branding approaches, 2012**

	Loyalty scheme branding	**Technical support branding**
Germany	Vodafone Stars	Net Guys
India	Vodafone Delights	Happy to help
Italy	Vodafone Top Club	Lab
UK	Freebee Rewardz	Tech Team

Godrej, an Indian conglomerate, however, manages its portfolio of businesses by pursuing growth in markets with similar consumer needs. For example, its hair-dye product, Expert, has been successful in countries as geographically far apart as India, South Africa, Argentina, Peru, Uruguay and Paraguay. Being able to sell the same product in different markets with familiar consumer needs and dynamics saves on research and development costs, reduces risk and reduces unit production costs as a result of greater volumes. Marketers should always look for new markets where consumers have similar needs and characteristics. It may result in a disparate collection of markets for a product, but, as in Godrej's case, increased efficiency and higher returns are more important than corporate neatness.

Balance risk and reward

Marketing investment in these types of opportunities needs to align with the company's overall business strategy and vision. But most global firms want to expand low-growth and high-growth opportunities at the same time, which involves marketing investment choices. Marketers must therefore calculate how much investment in time, money and other resources will be needed in a core market where the brand is established to maintain its sales and defence against competitors. Equally, how much will be required to establish the brand in a growing market and capture new customers who will be its future lifeblood?

Marketing investment allocation between the core and newer or developing markets should include a review of current and likely future revenues and profitability. Typically, current revenues and profitability come mainly from core markets and future revenues and profits depend much more on growth markets that hopefully will become core. A detailed assessment of when to shift investment more towards growth markets will depend on analysing past growth rates for each market and the market growth rate as a whole to see if the business is achieving growth that is faster or slower than market growth.

The most effective marketing investment strategies adopt a "release as you grow" approach for opportunities. This means that an investment based on potential growth is agreed. If the business growth exceeds this, further funds will become available. It is an incentive approach based on performance that creates investment transparency for the business and drives higher performance from marketing teams. The worst decision that can be made is to spread the marketing investment too thinly across too many markets and fail to achieve success in any. Targeting is essential.

Summary

There are many ways to grow markets and each requires a structured assessment. For chief marketing officers there are many demands on the marketing budget, and it is easy to dilute marketing effectiveness by spreading investment too thinly across too many opportunities. The decisions made on strategy must weigh the potential risks, the scale of financial reward and the probability of achieving success. A balanced approach requires that growth in higher risk and reward markets is pursued in conjunction with growth in lower risk and reward markets. Marketing teams need to make sure that current customers are well served while also attracting new customers. Any growth strategy must look at both the short term and the longer term.

6 Proposition definition

A BRAND PROPOSITION summarises why someone should buy a specific brand, product or service. It is an amalgamation of the brand's functional and emotional benefits and should convince a potential customer that this particular brand of product or service will fit their needs or delight them better than other brands' offerings will.

The brand proposition is central to a brand owner's growth strategy. It crystallises what the brand's competitive advantage is and what its appeal to customers is – that is, why they pay for it. It enables higher pricing or it assures customer loyalty – as is the case when low price is part of the proposition. In mature markets it establishes clear differentiation and increases preference for the brand over the competition, therefore increasing the share of a customer's total spend. In emerging markets and for new customers, it helps communicate relevance and therefore increases consideration and purchase of the brand. For existing customers, it validates their choice and establishes the reason to continue choosing the brand. It also clarifies the benefit that advocates of the brand will use as they spread the word about its virtues.

A brand makes a statement about a product – and makes purchasing decisions easier because it reduces the complexity to a few memorable phrases. For example:

- BMW is the ultimate driver's machine.
- Audi represents German technical superiority.
- Mercedes is elegant and powerful.

These companies' cars are similar in terms of features, engine performance, seating, styling, finish and price. The brand proposition is created to help customers choose between them. The different propositions are intended to appeal to slightly different types of customer, albeit those who want a premium, well-made German car. Each brand proposition emphasises a slightly different benefit that helps explain why it might be better for a particular customer. So it is also true to say that the statement the brand makes says as much about the brand user as it does about the brand itself. The most successful brands are able to manage the brand perceptions of their target customers. But the challenge they face is that they are not in total control of these perceptions because the phrases and word associations reside in customers' minds.

Customers are also influenced by a wide range of external forces; they care about the perceptions of friends and family, media imagery and style arbiters to confirm their opinions (this is covered in more detail in Chapter 9). The job of marketers is to form and then reinforce specific brand connotations to create and then strengthen consumer preference for the brand. Do Won Chang, the founder of Forever 21, an American fashion brand, with his daughters Esther and Linda (creative director and head of marketing respectively), would probably be happy with a teenage girl describing the brand as "hot" because it is an accurate enough interpretation of its brand proposition. But "mainstream" would be a worrying description for a brand engaged in selling young people the latest fashions cheaply and changing its inventory daily, as it would imply that it is losing its edge in the eyes of its target market.

Marketers talk variously about brand propositions and positioning, sometimes not differentiating between the two. Positioning is the market positioning or the relative positioning of a brand to other brands in the market rather than an overall proposition to customers. A relative positioning might explain that Target is slightly more expensive than the Walmart brand in the American superstore category, but it will not fully explain the brand proposition. The Target brand proposition communicates more reasons why Target might be more relevant and differentiating for a particular customer. Virgin Atlantic positions itself as a plucky upstart compared with, say, American Airlines or British Airways. The Virgin Atlantic brand proposition offers customers the benefit of joyful travel compared with BA's more functional "to fly to serve" proposition. This David and Goliath approach to market positioning has helped many brands grow, as consumers generally believe that the "small guy" cares more about them. Spicejet, a low-cost Indian airline, competes effectively with the incumbent Air India using this tactic.

These market positionings are important but they need to be based on customer insight to be truly compelling and relevant. In their book *Positioning: The Battle for Your Mind*, the chief tactic that Al Ries and Jack Trout recommend is to find some aspect of the product or service that is genuinely unique. That may mean recreating a category, or more easily subdividing it and being the best in that subdivision. For example, Instagram, a social-networking website bought by Facebook in 2012 for $1 billion, was successful because instead of trying to offer all forms of social networking it focused purely on photograph sharing. This may seem limiting, but Instagram created a subdivision within the social-networking category focusing on the value it could add to the existing photo-sharing trend. Everyday snaps could be – and still are – shared directly via Twitter and Facebook, but Instagram offered filters and editing capabilities that turned the average photo into a vintage work of art as well as flattering the user's photographic ability. This provided clear differentiation for Instagram that led to its category leadership. More impressive is that Instagram was not the first mover. It effectively usurped its predecessor, Hipstamatic, which offered similar photographic functionality but remained focused on the apps market. Hipstamatic's problem was that despite being one of only a few apps to offer this functionality, it did not focus on a brand proposition beyond being one of many thousands of apps in Apple's App Store. Instagram defined its brand proposition to consumers' widest need – sharing photos through social media – and then developed a niche within it, thus demonstrating the benefits of being a big fish in a small pond.

Different proposition strategies

Generating commercial growth through brand marketing relies on three factors:

- customer relevance;
- competitive differentiation;
- company authenticity.

Each customer segment will attach different weight to each of these. It is the job of marketers to strike the right balance.

Customer relevance

Brand propositions depend upon insight into customers and their needs: what single benefit customers most value, for example. But this raises the question of "which customer?". The most powerful propositions come from a fresh insight about a specific customer segment or an unmet need. Marketers undertake extensive research to identify unique insights. This may include ethnographic research techniques such as getting customers to fill in a diary about how they feel when using a product, or by observing customers in real life while they use it – for example, brushing their teeth or cooking a pizza at home. Such research provides real-life, qualitative insights into customers' needs and their likes and dislikes about a brand. In the washing-powder category, brands such as Omo (Persil), Ariel and Fairy try to express different benefits that are relevant to different target customers. These brands' marketing messages communicate different benefits that appeal to different customers:

- Omo (Persil) – "Dirt is good; Omo's unique technology gives your family the freedom to get dirty, safe in the knowledge that Omo will remove those awkward stains"
- Ariel – "Gives you brilliant results even under tough conditions. It leaves your wash brilliantly clean and your whites bright"
- Fairy – "Gives you amazingly clean clothes, soft towels and bedding, all with that gentle feeling of softness next to precious skin"

An important part of the marketing role is to make sure that the brand remains relevant as customer needs and expectations change. For example, Crest toothpaste has been around since the mid-1950s and the brand message originally focused on the product's therapeutic benefits as the first toothpaste that contained fluoride, a chemical compound that helps prevent tooth decay. In the 1960s the message changed and Crest was promoted on its cavity-prevention capability; since then other benefits have been included in the brand proposition, such as tartar prevention, fresh breath and whitening. More recently the focus has been on oral care, its ability to improve health rather than simply prevent decay, and the range now extends to mouthwashes, brushes and dental equipment. The Crest brand's ingredients and format have been updated, as has the brand proposition, to make sure that customers continue to choose it; as a result, it has had a fairly constant 30% market share in the United States throughout its long life.

Competitive differentiation

Several brands may be relevant to a customer's needs, so differentiating what a brand has to offer compared with competing brands is critical. Through highlighting the points of difference – the distinctive features of a brand – marketers can help make sure that the brand message is heard above all the surrounding marketing noise and distraction.

"Cut through" is the term often used by advertising agencies when talking about getting the brand message across; quite simply, it helps separate the message from the sea of similar messages about a product category. For example, both McDonald's and Burger King claim to use high-quality beef in their burgers, so customers have no reason to choose one or the other simply on the basis of the beef they use. Such points of parity may be relevant to consumers, but they do not help in differentiating two competing brands. A point of difference, by contrast, gives a consumer a reason to choose one brand over the other. For example, Burger King uses the slogan "Taste is King" linked to the "flame-grilled" cooking method to differentiate itself. McDonald's emphasises emotional benefits in its communications – "I'm lov'in it" – and provides free Wi-Fi in most of its restaurants. In practice, brands need both points of parity and points of difference, the former to help establish their relevance to consumers, and the latter to give consumers a reason to prefer them. A brand that is different without being relevant has little point. The commercial value of a brand lies in being able to emphasise its "relevant difference". And the extent of being able to do this is intrinsically linked to the depth of understanding there is of the customer's world and needs.

Strong brands polarise the market because they have loyal and profitable followers and advocates, while being unappealing to people outside the target audience. Coca-Cola and Pepsi Cola have long been rivals in the soft drinks market. Each seeks to provide a different proposition to customers so that they are loyal to only one brand. Pepsi loyalists in India, for example, ask for their favoured drink by name, "I'd like a Pepsi", rather than the generic "cola". The two brands have spent decades and many millions of dollars trying to be the number one global brand, despite the fact that they taste similar and in blind tasting tests consumers get confused about which brand they prefer. The brands have become an emblem of attitude and group belonging, just like Nike and Adidas. Their products offer little differentiation in terms of performance but present very different attitudes towards sport and fashion. The highly visible logos on these products allow customers to demonstrate a specific brand allegiance. Nike has long associated its brand with superstar American athletes such as LeBron James, Michael Jordan and Tiger Woods to create performance credibility, while Adidas has built more fashion credentials through its association with Stella McCartney.

Customers form such attachments to brands on the basis of the brand differentiators. The stronger the appeal of the differentiator, the stronger is the attachment – not unlike human relationships. Customers who become fans of the brand are usually incredibly loyal, easier and therefore less costly to serve, and have a higher customer lifetime value. They are likely to be strong advocates of the brand, providing in effect free advertising by spreading the word about its virtues. Lastly, and importantly, they will be tolerant – up to a point. Every brand has dips in performance, especially service brands. Brand loyalists are usually accommodating of minor aberrations. When the iPhone 5 was first released there was a problem with its map function. For another brand this kind of technical weakness could have been disastrous, but because Apple has such a powerful fan base, its customers in the main accepted the glitch as a rare aberration. However, if these types of mistakes continue to be made, Apple's brand will be weakened.

Brands are able to generate strong attachment to them when they have clear positioning from the start. British Airways started from the position of being the national airline with little or no competition; Virgin started with a clear vision of its target customers and the kind of airline "personality" that would appeal to them.

Company authenticity

As well as demonstrating its relevance and differentiating itself from the competition, a brand must be perceived as authentic to those both inside and outside the business. Authenticity is crucial to establishing trust in a brand. Proven expertise in a product category, area of technology or customer service will help establish the credibility that customers increasingly look for in a brand, and in today's digital world it is easy to access the information that will enable anyone to assess a company's credibility. That Toyota and BMW have invested heavily in green engineering technologies and manufacturing plants gives credibility to cars such as the Toyota Prius and BMW's range of Efficient Dynamics cars. Conversely, a marketing message that emphasises green credentials that are not supported by substantive evidence risks being seen as superficial, even dishonest, thus reducing overall trust in the brand.

Service brands are especially vulnerable to inauthentic behaviour by their employees that does not reflect the brand proposition. So employees need to be fully engaged in and supportive of the brand proposition if they are to behave in an authentic way towards customers. Employees will not – arguably, cannot – consistently provide an authentic on-brand experience if they do not believe in the brand proposition. Fred Smith, founder of FedEx, a global delivery services company, once claimed "It's People, Service, Profit, not Profit, Service, People", highlighting the importance of getting a team to believe in the vision.

Authenticity is also about what the firm can excel at. Could BMW credibly provide fast food? It has many professional abilities but no track record of any skill in that area. Customers would understandably not trust it to suddenly switch into catering. Dyson transformed the household vacuum-cleaner market and is now a highly successful multinational company. The insight of its founder, James Dyson, was that bag technology was inefficient and there had to be a better way of engineering vacuum cleaners. The Dyson brand proposition focuses on engineering design excellence delivering significantly better performance. This laid the ground for Dyson products to enjoy a huge price premium, often retailing at more than double the price of traditional cleaners. Subsequent diversification into other premium-price products has been patchy. Washing machines failed because they did not noticeably wash clothes any better. Airblade hand driers have been a great success because they perform so well. Keeping true to what was a clever and distinctive brand proposition has enabled the company to refine existing products, develop new ones, charge higher prices than its competitors and stay ahead of them.

However irresistible the temptation to "update" or "refresh" the brand proposition may seem, it is not always wise to do so. Many companies have been built on a great insight that may still hold true today and that is at the core of the brand proposition. InterContinental Hotels began life as part of Pan Am, an airline company that opened up the world for regular travellers with new routes. Pan Am quickly realised that these travellers needed places to stay once they arrived, so it set up InterContinental to build and run hotels at stop-off points on these routes. Pan Am went bust in 1991, but InterContinental is still going strong. Its brand proposition of being the "In the know" hotel with local knowledge at each destination authentically reflects its original purpose. Such authenticity is often described as the DNA of a brand – the internal truths that make it competitive, such as Coca-Cola's "refresh the world" or Nike's "just do it". Tempted as they may be to make their mark, new chief executives should always pause for thought before embarking on any dramatic modification of a brand's DNA. When succession takes place, staying true to the DNA ensures that the business is not driven off course by changes in personnel. But that is not the same as saying that the brand strategy may need to change in order to adapt to changing market circumstances, as Kodak and Nokia failed to recognise as the market for camera film was destroyed by digital cameras and as the smartphone market emerged.

Defining a proposition statement

There are several approaches to what should be in a proposition statement. FMCG brands favour a statement that is all-encompassing and covers relevance, the differentiated benefits and the brand's authenticity. Service brands generally emphasise only one of these three elements to keep the message simple and make sure that it resonates with all their typically wider range of customer segments. As David Still, head of brand strategy at Vodafone, says:

> Firstly, it's important to make sure you have all your key stakeholders involved right from the start, then keep the whole process and output as simple as possible; the simpler it is, the more likely non-marketing people in the organisation are to get it.

A brand proposition should identify the customer segment and express three core elements, for example: "For young adults, washing power X is the most reliable solution for washing clothes – it simplifies doing laundry because it combines new technology with proven efficient Y formula." The three elements are:

- what the product does – "combines new technology with proven efficient Y formula";
- how it delivers – "simplifies doing laundry";
- what the benefit is for customers – "the most reliable solution for washing clothes".

All these elements can work for any business, but those at the "benefit" end of the spectrum have more intangible value and are thus harder to replicate. They should, therefore, deliver higher commercial value to the business when properly implemented.

What the brand does

Some brands have a proposition that simply describes what they do for customers (see Figure 6.1). These are typically functional benefits such as the whitest cleaning toothpaste, the quickest car, or the slimmest smartphone. They are factual, easily measured and judged by customers against competitors' claims. They are also the easiest for competitors to overcome. If a competitor produces a slightly quicker

FIG 6.1 **Some brand propositions**

Brand	Brand proposition	Advertising slogan
McDonald's	Simple, easy, enjoyment	I'm lovin' it
British Airways	Thoughtful service that makes flying special for everyone	To fly, to serve
Audi	Sporty, progressive, sophisticated	*Vorsprung Durch Technik* (Progress though technology)
InterContinental Hotels	For people who want to be in the know, InterContinental is the brand that goes out of its way to deliver authentic and enriching experiences that make your world feel bigger	In the know

Sources: McDonald's; British Airways; Audi; InterContinental Hotels Group

car it negates the original brand proposition, with potentially serious commercial consequences. Functional benefits typically offer low value because they are rarely unique for long, making it difficult to maintain a price premium with this type of brand proposition.

How the brand benefits the customer

Many brand propositions communicate how the brand benefits customers. They give a sense of the personality of the brand. For example, Avis's "We try harder" suggests that the firm may not be the biggest or the best but its people work really hard to make the car rental experience special. McDonald's brand mission is "to be our customers' favourite place and way to eat and drink". It is committed to providing "high quality food and superior service in a clean, welcoming environment". This describes the clear benefits that customers can expect: high-quality food, superior service, great value and a welcoming and clean experience. Similarly, Accenture, a technology consulting firm, sells its brand on the phrase "high performance delivered".

These propositions are effective because they identify a single benefit that is defendable. HSBC's "The world's local bank" communicates the globally solid yet locally relevant nature of the bank. Hotel brand Ritz-Carlton's "Ladies and gentlemen serving ladies and gentleman" communicates that its well-heeled clientele can rest assured that they will be served by well-mannered staff.

Brand propositions that focus on emotional benefits usually resonate more with customers who are more likely to pay a higher price for the brand. They are also more likely to be loyal to the brand and therefore have a higher customer lifetime value for the firm. For example, Vodafone promotes an emotionally enabling benefit of "Power to you" compared with Nokia's more functional "Connecting people" message, which these days seems to say no more than what anyone would expect from a telecoms company, and so has become an undifferentiating benefit. Functional benefits are more easily replicated by competitors than emotional ones and are therefore less valuable for companies to own; the more intangible, higher-order benefits in Abraham Maslow's hierarchy of needs are more valuable precisely because they offer something emotional or aspirational as a benefit. (Maslow developed an often-used framework of human needs in a 1943 paper, "A Theory of Human Motivation". This ranked human needs in order of importance; basic needs like shelter and food need to be satisfied before people will seek out higher-order needs such as friendship, respect or self-esteem.)

Higher purpose

The most valuable brand proposition statements are those that describe a higher purpose for society as much as for the firm. Jim Stengel, a former Procter & Gamble marketer, describes this phenomenon in his book *Grow: How Ideals Power Growth and Profit at the World's Greatest Companies*. He shows how brands that demonstrate a wider societal benefit satisfy customers more. Dove, a soap brand, has built its brand proposition around "The campaign for real beauty". It shifted its promotional emphasis from an idealised beauty to the "real" beauty of everyday people, building credibility through global research into different attitudes to real beauty to highlight that everyone is beautiful in their own way. Dove's use of real-size, real women rather than the usual size zero models was revolutionary. It also funds the Movement for Self-esteem, which aims to widen the definition of beauty and inspire girls and women to take great care of themselves.

Employees like working for businesses that have a higher purpose and to share that purpose. Psychological research suggests that people generally want to do something meaningful at work. This is particularly true of generation Y employees, those born between the late 1980s and early 2000s during a time when there was a marked increase in social and environmental consciousness. They recognise that they will probably have to work well into their 60s or even 70s and care more about the future society than other demographic segments such as generation X (those born between 1966 and 1977) or baby-boomers (those born between 1946 and 1965). They want to work for organisations that are genuinely engaged in making a difference as well as making money.

Higher-purpose brand propositions emotionally engage employees and customers with a cause they can feel part of. The greater meaning the brand proposition has, the greater satisfaction customers and employees get from the brand in their different ways. For marketers, this means using social pressure and other psychological arm-twisting based on a sound understanding of what determines the way those in the target market behave. Higher-purpose brand propositions are difficult to implement successfully. For service businesses, the higher purpose is critical because services need to engage and galvanise work colleagues to perform their role better and keep on doing it over time. Big brands such as Ford, Zurich and Vodafone have hundreds of thousands of employees around the world. The brand proposition needs to motivate and provide guidance for their actions and behaviours. A functional statement can tell them what to do, but it requires something more meaningful if colleagues are to take personal ownership of the brand and align their behaviour around it (see Chapter 8 for a discussion of internal growth levers).

IBM, although well-regarded as an IT business, sought to increase its relevance and differentiation through developing and executing a higher-purpose proposition. It set itself a much bigger goal than the installation of the IT infrastructure systems than it was currently providing. In its own words, "it turns out that being connected isn't enough". It therefore established a new vision for the company based on the idea of a "Smarter Planet". This new proposition moves IBM from being a technical installation company to one that is trying to help improve the planet through smarter answers to the world's problems.

IBM is developing IT systems that can transform the way that health care is provided by, for example, connecting global medical expertise with local children in Zambia as well as other systems that will ensure food arrives fresh in supermarkets with minimal wastage of resources. The championing of a cause – that the world can be a better place through more technologically advanced IT systems – helps the IBM brand stand out from its competitors and resonate more with a wide range of people and organisations. Research indicated that IBM's growth increasingly involved working with government policymakers. For example, it helped President Obama's team identify the benefits of smart infrastructure over traditional methods. These smart systems go beyond the simple record-keeping of traditional systems, identifying patterns in the data and therefore creating better solutions to managing patient health care, hospital facilities and amounts of drugs that are needed to cope with future population changes. IBM highlighted the fact that 900,000 jobs could be created by building smart systems health-care, IT and broadband businesses over the next five years.

When a business is claiming the high ground, it must genuinely occupy it – and proving that it does requires openness and transparency about sourcing and employment practices and, as has become clear, tax arrangements. Authenticity should be not just be in the marketing message; it must also permeate the whole organisation and all its activities.

Clarifying the proposition messages

A singular, overarching brand proposition helps guide the strategic direction of a firm. When it is kept simple and powerful it often becomes part of a firm's lexicon and aids corporate decision-making. It is easy to imagine managers at Volvo, a carmaker, referring to its stated mission of "quality, safety and environmental care", or those at Gillette checking that a new razor is, as its advertising claims, "the best a man can get". This is the value of a powerful, memorable brand proposition. But although this is good for the overall direction of the

FIG 6.2 **A message matrix**

Overall proposition	Live more with a specialist health-care partner			
Audience	**Consumers**	**SMEs**	**Corporates**	**Investors**
Primary message for each audience	Feel confident, be healthy	Healthy people, productive business	Drive employee attraction and productivity	Sustainable profitable growth
Three supporting messages	The expert health-care partner who can help you choose the right product	Expertise that delivers the best care for your whole team	Experts in reducing health risks and increasing your return on investment (ROI)	World-class management team with depth and breadth of experience
	Quick access to preferred treatment that's right for you	Flexible products at the right price	Partner with you to develop the right health-care strategy for your company	Patients' preferred provider for long-term health-care support
	Depth of experience delivering the best care and support	Straightforward to deal with	Breadth and depth of experience to deliver the best health-care for your employees	Above market ROI

firm, a proposition should be easy to translate into a series of sub-messages that communicate explicit benefits to specific audiences. This is particularly important because modern commerce has a wide range of stakeholding interests to take into account, including employees, partners, investors and influential opinion formers as well as customers.

The benefit of the type of proposition and message matrix illustrated in Figure 6.2 is that it helps marketers and managers think in terms of conversations, rather than one-way communications. In the past, companies simply shouted about their products, clearly outlining the key benefits and letting customers decide if they liked them. There was no attempt to seek customers' opinions or engage them in a two-way dialogue. With social media such as Twitter and Facebook it is now easy to engage customers in topics, encouraging them to share their views on a product and its benefits. AstraZeneca, a multinational pharmaceutical company, recently changed its marketing approach to one based on the brand vision of "Health connects us all". It is trying to demonstrate that it sees its purpose beyond simply making drugs to the more universal purpose in providing health care for everyone.

Higher-purpose propositions are more easily activated through conversations with all stakeholders because they are about an issue not a product. The message matrix helps marketers manage each of these conversations, which are naturally distinct, and link them back to IBM's ultimate brand proposition: a "Smarter planet".

This type of message matrix is also valuable in future scenario planning. Scenario plans are descriptions of different conditions and likely outcomes. For example, they might describe the investments and outcomes for low-growth or high-growth scenarios; or the different investments and outcomes of growth in China compared with India. This is particularly useful during a merger or acquisition as it is important to outline the benefit messages for each stakeholder group. In the past few years several insurance companies have demerged or sold off assets. AIG, an American insurance company, sold its Alico brand to MetLife, also an American insurance company, in 2010. ING, a Dutch multinational banking and financial services company, is demerging its American insurance business and launching it as a standalone brand called Voya on the New York Stock Exchange in 2014. As firms consider whether to sell to another firm or launch a new, separate brand, it is helpful to understand the shared and different messages that benefit the different audiences and business scenarios. When a brand is bought by another firm, as with Alico and MetLife, it is important to communicate the shared values, culture and growth. But when it is becoming standalone, like Voya, it is more important to communicate a sense of independence and optimism.

Marketing managers involved in demergers, sales of business units and acquisitions have found it helpful to draw up a matrix of potential benefits because these deals often change course over time. For example, a bank may try to sell an ailing business unit to another business (trade sale), or to an investment vehicle (sovereign wealth fund or private equity house), or to the management through a management buy-out, or directly to investors through an initial public offering (IPO). Flexibility and timing are needed to maximise returns. Thus having a comprehensive view of potential benefits for each scenario gives business leaders the greatest knowledge and power during the deal. To maximise its effectiveness, a brand proposition needs to be subtly tailored to each of these audiences and situations.

Summary

A brand proposition needs to be based on customer relevance and competitive differentiation, and to be authentic to the company. It should be enduring and reflect long-term strategy, but sub-messages can be varied and tailored for different segments. This helps to maintain an overarching brand proposition while increasing the effectiveness of marketing communications. The most compelling brand propositions are those that describe a higher purpose beyond the simple functionality of the product category they work in. This higher purpose offers employees, customers and partners a more emotional reason to choose this brand over another. The emotional benefit, if real and deep, is less easy to copy and more valuable, thus creating longer-term value for the organisation. The success of a brand proposition depends on it being consistently truthful. If it isn't, or if it is changed every few years, it will confuse customers and lose impact.

7 Brand portfolio growth

COMPANIES THAT OWN a number of different brands will be primarily interested in the value of, and return from, the whole portfolio rather than that of a single brand. A range of approaches and techniques can be used to help maximise the returns on the different brands and avoid one cannibalising the sales of another.

The starting point is clarity about the role of the corporate brand or company brand. For companies like HSBC, IBM and Apple the corporate brand is all. For Procter & Gamble, Diageo and Unilever it is the brands that they own rather than the corporate brand that matter most to consumers, though for suppliers and employees the corporate brand may be just as important as the brand business unit they supply or work for. For some of the world's most famous brands, such as Coca-Cola, the company's brand is the brand of its most famous product, but Coca-Cola also owns other brands such as Minute Maid, Fanta and Glaceau Vitamin Water, whose loyal fans may have no idea that their favourite drink brand is owned by Coca-Cola. Well-known firms like BMW, Google and IBM use their corporate brand as the overarching consumer-facing brand, or "master brand" as marketers call it. Beneath the master brand will be a range of other brands and sub-brands that make up the portfolio, The different types of brand that make up a portfolio fall into the following categories:

- corporate brand;
- master brand;
- product/proposition brand;
- sub-brand;

■ standalone brand;

■ own-label brand.

Those responsible for managing the portfolio have the job of making the whole add up to more than the sum of its parts, nurturing new brands, ensuring that established brands do not lose their edge and, where possible, using one brand or sub-brand to support and boost another. Audi, for example, uses its R8 high-performance car, TT sports car and Q7 sports utility vehicle (SUV) to validate its brand proposition of premium German engineering. This then provides the necessary "halo" to sell high volumes of more affordable but still premium-priced mid-range saloon cars.

Brand architecture is a term often used in the context of brand portfolio management, but in essence brand architecture can be reduced to the equivalent of an organisational chart showing how different brands and sub-brands fit into the corporate structure. Brand architecture reviews are generally more inward looking, emphasising corporate and visual neatness rather than the active management of brand assets to maximise customer growth potential. Designing the brand architecture is, therefore, much easier than managing the portfolio of brands that make up the architecture.

The role of the portfolio components

Corporate brands

Companies like IBM, HSBC and BMW have a portfolio strategy that is anchored to a single master brand, while others such as Unilever, Procter & Gamble and Diageo have a strategy based on a number of product-line brands in which the corporate brand has a low presence for consumers. However, the corporate brand has particular significance for investors, governments, business observers and employees, rather than consumers, and is the brand through which messages on such matters as corporate governance, financial performance and corporate social responsibility are communicated. The corporate brand supports a portfolio of consumer brands. For example, Procter & Gamble's stable of brands includes Tide, Pampers, Gillette and Braun; Unilever owns Dove, Cif and Persil; and Pfizer, a pharmaceutical company, has Lucozade, Advil and Centrum vitamins in its portfolio.

There is no right or wrong approach as all these successful companies have demonstrated. But the decision of which strategy to adopt is an important one. If a company wants to sell to a narrowly defined customer group such as wealthy managers a narrow product range such as premium cars, a master brand strategy is typically more effective. But if the range of customers and their needs and the company's range of propositions are more diverse, using a collection of brands may generate higher financial returns.

It is important to have a clear strategy for what the role of corporate brand is. There are two main choices:

■ it is primarily not consumer facing but has a range of strong consumer-facing brands, for example Procter & Gamble, Diageo and Unilever;

FIG 7.1 **Corporate brands: portfolio strategy and roles**

P&G *Procter & Gamble*	⋈ HILTON WORLDWIDE	Ⓜ Mercedes-Benz
House of brands	**Hybrid**	**Masterbrand**
Corporate brand is primarily for investors and employees with a portfolio of consumer-facing brands	Several brands linked by different types of verbal or visual connection to the master brand	Strong brand equity of master brand leveraged across different consumer propositions
Crest Duracell Fairy Gillette IAMS Oral B Pampers Pantene Tampax Tide Vicks	Hilton Hotels & Resorts Hilton Garden Inn Hilton Grand Vacations Doubletree by Hilton Hampton by Hilton Homewood Suites by Hilton Embassy Suites Conrad Waldorf Astoria Hilton Honours	Mercedes Benz A-Class Mercedes Benz B-Class Mercedes Benz C-Class Mercedes Benz CL-Class Mercedes Benz E-Class Mercedes Benz G-Class Mercedes Benz GL-Class Mercedes Benz M-Class Mercedes Benz S-Class Mercedes Benz SL-Class Mercedes Benz SLK-Class

Less similar customer needs and propositions — *More similar customer needs and propositions*

Sources: Procter & Gamble; Hilton Worldwide; Mercedes-Benz

FIG 7.2 **Procter & Gamble's consumer-facing brands**

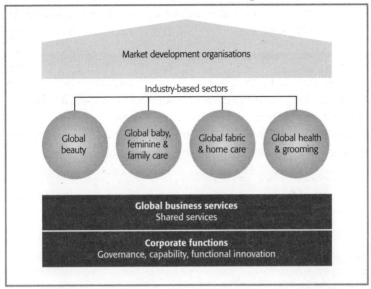

Source: PG.com

- it is the primary customer-facing master brand, for example Mercedes, HSBC and IBM.

A third option is a hybrid of the two, where the firm has a strong master brand as well as other, smaller sub-brands. An example is Hilton, which owns the main Hilton Hotels and Resorts brand, Hilton Garden Inn, Hilton Grand Vacations as well as the Doubletree, Hampton and Homewood suites brands that are endorsed by the Hilton brand. It also owns the standalone Embassy suites, Conrad hotels and Waldorf Astoria hotel brands as part of its hybrid portfolio (see Figure 7.1).

The benefit of operating with a collection of brands is that each brand can be more targeted towards specific customer segments with more tailored propositions. It also allows companies to operate a number of brands in the same categories and therefore increase market share in them. Meanwhile, economies of scale can be achieved by sharing back-office or production functions across a number of brands and through larger production volumes (see Figure 7.2).

A master-brand strategy requires maximising the relationship and role of the corporate brand with the customer-facing parts of the business. The potential benefits of a master-brand strategy are that:

- the entire marketing budget can be invested in building just one strong brand;
- it reduces confusion and makes it easier for consumers make brand choices;
- it increases cross-selling opportunities;
- it can bring greater cohesion and efficiency to its performance, not least through making it easier to share marketing best practices and thereby improve overall performance;
- it ensures a consistent – and therefore stronger – selling message.

Philips has a master-brand strategy with the Philips name covering a vast range of products from hairdryers and toasters to medical scanners and lighting. In 2006 the company phased out its only strong sub-brand, Philishave, and its shavers are now sold under the Philips master brand. In the United States it has also begun the process of strengthening its master-brand strategy by co-branding its American Norelco products Philips Norelco in preparation for phasing out the Norelco name.

Although master brands have a single name, they are usually used for a range of products or services, which will each shape customer perception to a different extent, with net brand asset "builders" and those that are supported by the overall master brand. Mercedes-Benz has a master-brand policy with products that use a simple alphabetical descriptor such as Mercedes-Benz C-Class, thus making sure that the master brand remains the most important branding element (see Figure 7.3). Consumer perceptions of the overall master brand are shaped by a few flagship products that highlight its brand essence, "power and elegance", as described in "Enduring passion, the story of the Mercedes-Benz brand". Its power credentials are clearly demonstrated by the $256,000 Mercedes-Benz SLS-AM, with a top speed of 199 miles per hour (mph) and an acceleration speed of 0–62 mph in 3.7 seconds. The company also uses its AMG performance-tuning service brand to reinforce performance perceptions. Most Mercedes–Benz cars have an AMG version, which uses higher specification engines

FIG 7.3 **Mercedes Benz's brand portfolio perception flows**

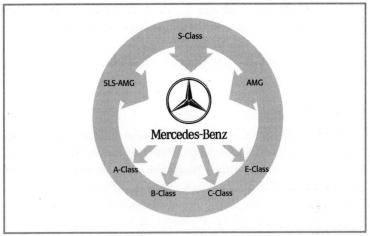

Source: Mercedes-Benz

and carbon-fibre materials to increase performance and handling compared with regular Mercedes models. AMG models are typically the most expensive and have the highest performance in each Mercedes class. Mercedes-Benz's "Elegance" brand perceptions are shaped by the luxury S-Class model, which is recognised as an industry leader in quality, sophistication and elegance. It is regularly voted the best saloon car in the world (its name, S-Class, is an abbreviation of *Sonderklasse* or special class). Many standard car features today, such as air bags, collision-proof fuel tanks, ABS braking and traction control systems, were first introduced by Mercedes-Benz on the S-Class. These models typically generate small sales volumes but high profits and build the overall master-brand perception, which filters through the range of more affordable cars that sell in large volumes with lower profits. This provides Mercedes Benz with an efficient and effective portfolio strategy that delivers optimal growth. Revenues increased by 7% in 2012, from $140 billion in 2011 to $151 billion, and net profits by 8%, from $7.9 billion in 2011 to $8.6 billion.

Marketers manage this relationship by adjusting the weight of marketing activity as the strength of the master brand's subsidiary brands flourish or struggle.

Business analysts and rating agencies often rate "clarity of strategy" highly on their assessment criteria, which encourages companies to favour master-brand strategies. But increasingly there is a view that a pure master-brand strategy carries a higher risk, not least because a scandal involving one product or business unit can damage the whole portfolio.

Product or proposition brands

Most master brands use product brands to sell individual offerings, for example BMW "3 Series" cars, HSBC "Premier" bank accounts, Panasonic "Viera" televisions. They should have memorable and distinctive names, but they also need to be coherent and highlight the overall scope of the firm as well as the benefits of specific types of product. For example, the BMW 3 Series car is obviously smaller than the 5 Series but larger than the 1 Series. The most effective benefit of product brands is that they do not detract too much from the master brand, as it is always clear that the most important element is the BMW name.

Sub-brands

Sub-brands are names and identities that are significantly distinct from the master brand and have a strong enough reputation that is recognised by consumers – though they still rely to a varying extent on the master brand to provide awareness and a reference point in the marketplace. Examples include: PlayStation (Sony), Fusion (Gillette), iPod and iPad (Apple) and DKNY (Donna Karan). As product brands become stronger and gain longevity, they may become sub-brands (by accident or intention). Sub-brands require careful management to make sure that they do not take value away from the master brand and that the most effective add value to the master brand as well. Sub-brands can generate high value in their own right by being partly separate, but ineffective management may cause customers to transfer their loyalty away from the master brand to the sub-brand, thereby reducing opportunities to cross-sell and decreasing overall sales.

Standalone brands

The reasons for creating a standalone brand include the need to:

- target a distinct customer base;
- target a non-core business area;
- sell a non-core proposition;
- build a partnership brand.

And when a well-known brand is acquired through a merger or acquisition it will usually be left as a standalone brand – as Rolls-Royce was when acquired by BMW and as YouTube was when bought by Google.

When Toyota realised its brand would not credibly stretch into the premium car market it launched the Lexus brand in 1989, after spending an estimated $1 billion on development costs and creating the new brand identity. It continues to invest heavily in Lexus and in promoting the brand, spending $324m on advertising in the United States in 2011 out of the total $1.06 billion advertising spend of the Toyota Group. Sales of the Lexus the United States now account for 4.6% of Toyota's global unit sales.

Standalone brands have no visible connection with the master brand, operating with separate sales, distribution channels and marketing campaigns, and therefore require a significant investment to launch and manage.

Own-label brands

These are brands that are created typically by retailers to provide an alternative to established brands in a category; in time they become established in their own right. Tesco has extensive own-label ranges including "Finest", a range of higher-priced products, and "Value", a range of lower-priced products. They are designed to embody the values of the supermarket brand to compete with the leading brands in each category and represent a large proportion of their total sales. For Aldi, a German discount retailer, this is 94%, while for Tesco it is 38% and for Sainsbury's 20%. Compared with any single product brand these own-label brands are a formidable force, with Tesco's

Finest brand delivering over $1.5 billion in revenues in the UK alone in 2012.

The advantages to retailers of own-label brands include:

- more control over the ingredients, flavour or materials of the product that is designed to their own specification;
- greater cross-selling opportunities as own-label ranges span more categories than other brands;
- full control over the marketing of the products whereas other brands come with their own advertising and promotions;
- the ability to capitalise on the trend of changing customer preference towards own-label ranges in the belief that the quality is reasonable but better value than non-retailer brands. This is particularly true in a recession where shoppers are more price conscious; Mintel research confirms that own-label sales in the UK have grown on average 4.8% each year since 2006.

US retailer Target relaunched its own-label brand as "Up & Up" with an expanded product selection and a new design. Up & Up carries over 1,000 product offerings across 67 categories and it claims that its products are of equal quality to well-known brands at a fraction of the cost – an average saving of 30%. In the fast-moving consumer goods arena, many competing brands have responded to the own-brand threat by focusing on the brand proposition (see Chapter 6) and delivering added value through online sales promotions.

Brand architecture

Brand architecture is a term used to describe the structuring and naming of all of a company's products and services. Like an organisational chart, the structure helps customers understand the scope of a company's products and choose one that suits them. Clear brand architecture groups together products with similar benefits, such as the Porsche brand's Cayenne SUV, 911 two-seat sports car and Pannemera four-seat saloon car. Within each of these groups there are also several varieties of engine size, performance and interior materials quality to choose from.

Names and looks

The naming and visual identity (the logo and related visual aspects of the brand) of branded products and services and the way that they are visualised has a huge impact on perceptions of the brand and all the products associated with it. There should be a clear naming convention for brand portfolios. BMW, for example, has an alphanumeric system: BMW 1 Series, BMW 2 Series, BMW 3 Series, and so on. Apple uses a series of names mostly with an 'i' prefix: iPad, iPod, iTunes and iPhone. Both brands have a clear way or convention for creating new names that fit with the current portfolio. The benefits of a consistent and clear product-naming convention message across all the products in the portfolio are that it:

- keeps things simple;
- reduces customer confusion;
- allows resources to be focused on a single brand;
- facilitates new product launches.

Names can vary from the functionally descriptive like British Airways or Bank of America to the more abstract like Starbucks or the Nintendo "Wii" electronic games console. The choice of name often depends on factors such as how serious or light-hearted the product is. Making sure the tone is appropriate and that the perception created by the name is in tune with the brand proposition is crucial.

There is also the matter of investment cost – for example, how much of the overall marketing budget is available to invest in establishing and growing a distinctive new brand name? Bank of America provides an easy descriptor for its type of services, requiring little marketing investment. By contrast, Nintendo's Wii brand required a lot of investment to build name recognition, but as a result it now provides much greater differentiation from competitors' products.

Using a consistent visualisation of the product names helps to create clarity across a range of different product offerings because they are easier for customers to recognise and compare with each other. BMW uses the same font for each of its product names across the range; BMW 3-Series, BMW 5-Series and BMW 7-series to help customers understand the relationship between different cars in the range. Other car companies create different logos for different cars but this reduces the overall coherence and makes it more difficult to understand the range. The Ford Fiesta has a heavy handwritten style visual while the Ford Focus uses a clean, san-serif font. This all adds costs and does not make it easier for customers to instinctively gauge each car's position in the range.

For international companies, the decision on whether to use a single global language (usually English) or the local language in different markets can be difficult. The sector that the business is involved in can be the determining factor. Technology and banking are two sectors where a single English brand name is generally used worldwide. In fashion, cosmetics and food, the decision is not so simple, and customer research is often carried out to provide insight into what will work best. For example, Carrefour, a large global retailer, uses Chinese characters for its name in China which means "home + happiness + lucky"; whereas Samsung, an electronics company, uses the same English word in every market.

The brand portfolio management process and tools

It is important to have simple guidelines for managing a portfolio of brands, especially in global organisations with many hundreds of marketers making thousands of decisions that affect the value of the portfolio. In considering any addition to the brand portfolio, there needs to be an assessment first of the current portfolio, and second of what the customer needs are in the target business sector and what kind of competitor brands and sub-brands are already serving those customers and their needs. These questions can be answered using a set of assessment criteria as shown in Table 7.1. Rigorous data and insights from colleagues who work on each brand will help provide the most accurate answers to these questions.

Assessment

The main factors to consider are the scope of the customer opportunity, the current equity of the brand, strategic fit with the business and the potential economic contribution. Answers to these questions can be arrived at using statistical analysis or simply by allowing managers

TABLE 7.1 **Portfolio management assessment criteria**

Main factors	Detailed assessment criteria
What is the size of customer opportunity?	Is the primary customer target growing or shrinking? What are the primary customer needs? Is brand highly relevant to these customers and the category?
What is the current brand equity of the brand(s)?	What is the brand awareness? What are the main brand attributes, both positive and negative? Is the brand highly differentiated from the competition? Is the brand highly differentiated from the competition? Which part of the brand is driving the purchase decision: master brand or product brand? What is the price perception of the brand?
What is the strategic fit?	How well does it fit with business and brand objectives now and in the future? What role does the corporate brand play in the portfolio? Does it help the firm to access new customers, markets or product categories?
What is the economic contribution?	Satisfactory revenues and margins? Sustainable future revenues and margins? Good return on investment on marketing spend? What are the growth and brand extension opportunities in the next 3–5 years?
What is the growth potential?	Which brands can add value to other brands in the portfolio? Can the brand be extended beyond the current product or customer base?

to use their experience and judgment. For an organisation with a master-brand strategy, using a decision tree of questions to which there is only a yes or no answer can be a helpful part of the evaluation process and is often used in the context of acquisitions when deciding whether to keep a separate brand or merge it into the master brand (see Figure 7.4). For example, BMW kept Mini, Bentley and Rolls-Royce as a sub-brands, as Amazon did with LoveFilm and Audible.

If the data are available, it is possible to calculate the potential financial gains from any change to the portfolio and compare different risk–reward options. The use of such analysis gives marketers a stronger hand in the shaping and management of the portfolio. Creating a

FIG 7.4 **A decision-tree tool for managing portfolio decisions**

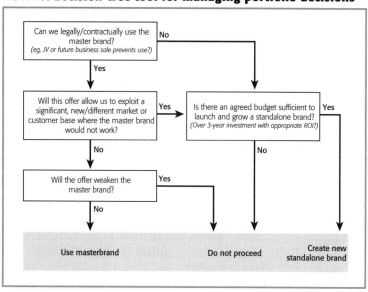

business and brand opportunity map like the one shown in Figure 7.5 helps explore the different options. The business growth value for each part of the portfolio is taken from the company's standard three-year financial forecast report. This is the company's profit forecast figure for each of the portfolio elements. The brand analysis figure should reflect the strength of each brand element in the portfolio. The data can come from a variety of sources, such as brand image or brand strength consumer research that the company may undertake on an annual basis, or net promoter scores (see Chapter 2) for each part of the portfolio. The size of each circle represents the future value of revenues for each portfolio element. The map therefore gives a clear picture of which of the portfolio elements have the highest profit potential, the largest value of revenues and the strongest brands.

Deciding what to change

Using a matrix along the lines of the BCG growth-share matrix (see Chapter 5) will help in the reshaping of the portfolio strategy and in categorising the role of each brand and sub-brand in relation to its

FIG 7.5 **Brand portfolio value and risk analysis matrix**

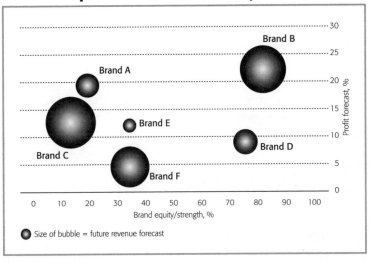

Size of bubble = future revenue forecast

FIG 7.6 **Brand portfolio definition tool**

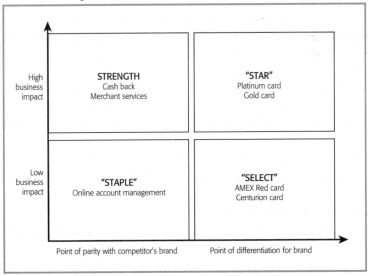

contribution to the portfolio. It also helps separate the brand elements or products that provide a point of difference from the competition and those that merely match it. It provides a more detailed definition than the initial brand assessment map (see Figure 7.5) as it can include all the brand elements and products or services. Thus the matrix can act as a useful organising tool for the portfolio by providing a clear overview and showing where the opportunities for greatest marketing investment and return lie. It also assigns a type of brand descriptor to each quadrant (see Figure 7.6).

Star

Star products and services have high impact on commercial results and are strong brand differentiators. American Express's Centurion and Platinum cards are heavily used by high earners and provide differentiation from other high-street banks' cards. The Centurion card, launched in 1999, is black and is made of titanium. It creates a great brand image of exclusivity and service, as it is an invitation-only card that has no set purchase limit. It provides customers with a range of exclusive concierge services. Stars are a portfolio's most powerful brands and generate a significant proportion of a firm's profits. They are a valuable asset and merit the investment required to protect and maintain their performance.

Select

Select products and services are highly differentiated but may in themselves deliver lower commercial benefits. They are frequently used by marketers to create a halo across the entire portfolio and can grow into stars. American Express uses its Red card to draw attention to its social enterprise activities, attracting socially conscious consumers and demonstrating the company's wider moral commitment to society. Select offerings are best used to emphasise a specific attribute or benefit of the brand or to target an influential segment. Audi successfully uses its Audi R8 sports car to demonstrate its high-performance credentials and cast a halo of performance across its more ubiquitous family cars. It may sell few R8 cars, but the impact on the overall brand helps sell millions of family cars, providing revenues and profits for the firm.

Strength

Products and services that bring in substantial revenues albeit at low margins help attract customers to the brand and increase overall awareness. American Express offers a Basic card with no annual fee and no interest charges as long as customers pay off the debt each month. There are no additional benefits such as reward points or brand benefits of the Red card, but it provides an entry-level card for large numbers of customers. Such product variations should have descriptive names that help customers select the product variation that is most appropriate for them but make sure that the primary attachment is to the master brand.

Staple

Staples are usually simple components of products or services. American Express offers its customers online account management, but this is a feature of its standard cards and should not have a specific brand name. It is intrinsic to the overall service and expected from a major credit-card provider. Marketers are often tempted to highlight every feature of a service by creating separate trademarked names for them. This undermines the clarity of the offers and dilutes the strength of the master brand. Naming every component is also expensive and time-consuming and provides little additional trademark protection.

Adjusting the portfolio strategy

The brand portfolio matrix is helpful in portfolio management but it should be revisited regularly and revised as necessary with corresponding adjustments to the portfolio strategy and its implementation. Tata, an Indian conglomerate, owns the Jaguar and Land Rover brands in its automotive portfolio, but the product portfolio choices it made following their acquisition in 2000 helped it achieve stronger financial results. It consolidated its position in the premium SUV market by refining and relaunching the Range Rover, a star product. This offered customers even greater luxury and comfort and increased sales by 14,120 units in 2011–12. A new sub-brand, the Range Rover Evoque, was introduced at a much lower price than the Range Rover. This was the smallest, lightest and most fuel-efficient

Range Rover yet and helped increase positive brand perceptions with a new range of more cost-conscious customers. In its first year the Evoque added an additional 20.6% to the total sales of Tata's Jaguar Land Rover division. The Range Rover Discovery, a strength product, continued to sell well, increasing by 6,200 units in 2011–12. The Jaguar XF car was launched in 2008 to extend the range and compete against the BMW 5-Series. In 2009 the Jaguar XJ was relaunched and in 2012 came the announcement of a new sub-brand, the Jaguar F-type, a sports car designed to emphasise the speed and glamour of historical Jaguars.

There is boldness in the Jaguar Land Rover division's approach to its portfolio strategy; two new sub-brands were added, the Range Rover Evoque and Jaguar F-type, and the existing portfolio of products was improved. All these portfolio choices demonstrate an active management of the portfolio to make the most of new growth opportunities through a strong and coherent range of products. This has resulted in large increases in sales to new customers as well as products that generate higher margins and therefore increase total company profits, as described later in this chapter.

Sometimes companies introduce a new feature with little fanfare because it is assumed it will have little benefit. However, consumers may become delighted with it and the feature becomes a significant hit for the company. The portfolio management issue is whether to reinforce the brand name, upgrading it to strength or star to guarantee maximum protection for what is now a highly prized commercial asset. McDonald's upgraded its coffee offer from a generic product called simply coffee to one named "Full Bean Coffee" to strengthen its role in the overall brand portfolio. This strategic shift has two benefits: it demonstrates an improved coffee product to compete more effectively with chains such as Starbucks; and it provides McDonald's with a tangible portfolio strength, increasing quality perceptions for the overall brand.

Brand extension

Brand extensions are introduced to generate new revenue streams and increase a brand's overall profitability. The Dove brand began life as single product – a women's moisturising soap – and has been successfully extended across a wide range of female personal-care products and male personal care, including shower gel, soaps and moisturisers. This kind of extension is successful when it stays true to the original attributes of the initial product. It needs to be credible to the consumer, the brand and the company. When executed successfully it can create a powerful presence in the stores and help dominate a category, as consumers begin to buy several products from the same brand. This is less risky than launching an entirely new brand because the company knows that it already has customers who like and buy it. It is much easier to sell a similar product to the same customer than try to find new customers or build a new brand from scratch. The danger is the temptation to extend the brand to products that, when launched, consumers do not find a credible fit with the brand – a stretch too far, in other words. There are three strategies for brand extension:

- extend the consumer audience;
- extend the product category;
- extend the brand proposition.

Audience extension

Extending the consumer audience means simply convincing more consumers that the brand is a credible choice, encouraging them to switch from their current preferred product. The growth techniques described in Chapter 4 cover this.

Product category extension

Extending the product category is the most used approach and is covered in detail in Chapter 5. It achieves commercial growth by launching products in adjacent categories that existing customers will find attractive. This might mean buying a Mercedes sports car to complement a Mercedes family car or buying a L'Oréal hair dye to match the L'Oréal shampoo and hairspray. This is attractive to consumers because:

- they already trust the brand and product experience, so it offers lower risk;

- they may perceive that products of the same brand will work better together than products of different brands, so a Gillette post-shave moisturiser will work better with Gillette shaving foam than another brand;

- the product features will generally work in the same way so it is easier to learn. If a family member owns a Samsung Galaxy S smartphone, other family members will benefit from choosing Samsung phones because they have similar operating systems.

Some consumers may feel that there is a financial benefit – that is, purchasing a collection of products is cheaper than purchasing the products individually because the company has achieved some production synergies and efficiencies.

Brand proposition extension

The brand proposition was covered in detail in Chapter 6. When embarking on an extension to the proposition, the core brand attributes must retain the strength and authenticity that are derived from its current attributes. However, it is possible to extend the scope of the core brand through additional attributes provided they too are strong and authentic. For example, the Volvo brand's primary proposition has long been safety, but it has been extended to include attributes of style and design. Similarly, the McDonald's brand has been extended beyond convenience to take account of health and social concerns through, in practice, the use of 100% beef, fair-trade partnerships and healthier menu options.

Premium and value brand extensions

One of the biggest challenges in portfolio management is how to extend the range of products to a higher or lower price through premium and value ranges. Customers typically view a brand as belonging to a specific price bracket; for example, Giorgio Armani is a luxury fashion brand, Lenovo is a mid-priced electronics brand and Kia is budget car brand. While all have variants in the range of what they sell, most of their products are within the price bracket they are associated with. If the owners want to extend the price range for these brands, they must decide whether the master brand will stretch far enough away from the existing price range.

Extending upmarket

Extending a brand upmarket is difficult without spending a great deal of time and money on marketing. The existing master brand will lack the credibility to deliver a superior product in a more expensive market. When Volkswagen launched its premium Phaeton car it became the flagship for the entire VW range at $82,000. It was designed to help VW compete with BMW and Mercedes and was built from the same engineering base as the Bentley Continental, which cost around $184,000. However, despite the capacity to build 20,000 cars a year, it sold only around a quarter of that number. Sales in the United States were so bad that Volkswagen stopped selling the Phaeton there in 2006. The problem was not the car, which had been well reviewed by motoring journalists. The problem was the brand – customers just did not perceive VW as a premium car brand. As a UK magazine, *What Car?*, confirmed in 2013: "The Volkswagen Phaeton's execution is faultless, but the VW badge simply isn't desirable enough to compete in this class."

The premium customers that VW was targeting did not want to be associated with a mid-market brand, however good value it was. An effective brand portfolio strategy needs to make sure that there is a clear distinction between the new premium brand or sub-brand and the original master brand. This means that the new brand, its products and distribution channels will fit perfectly with the new target customers' needs. It also helps avoid stretching the master brand range to where it begins to lack credibility with either audience. Unlike Volkswagen, Toyota and Nissan achieved sales in the premium car market by introducing new brands to their portfolios, the Lexus (Toyota) and Infiniti (Nissan), to gain more premium customers at higher prices. Both these brands have grown successfully, with Toyota selling over 500,000 Lexus cars in 2012.

To make a success of extending a brand upmarket there are a number of strategies that marketers can attempt:

- Use a clear premium brand and descriptor, such as HSBC's Premier bank account or British Airways' Gold loyalty card and First Class cabin.

- Make sure that there is a clear product specification difference between the premium and the normal range.

- Use a distinct sales channel. Apple and Sony have built their own retail outlets dedicated to their products to make sure that they are displayed and sold in an appropriately upmarket way. They have full control of these outlets so that everything emphasises the brand proposition.

- Co-brand with a luxury partner. Siemens created a range of domestic appliances with a designer, F.A. Porsche. The stainless-steel coffee-makers and toasters were branded "Siemens by Porsche Design". Their distinctive design meant that these higher-priced products were perceived as superior to Siemens's normal ranges of appliances.

- Create a price gap (rather than overlap) between the most expensive mid-range product and the lowest-priced premium product.

Extending downmarket

This is a more frequently used means of seeking to gain more customers because it requires less marketing investment and has more chance of success. Customers are more likely to accept that a premium brand can make a cheaper version of a product than that a budget brand can make a premium version. This is because people believe that it requires more skill to make an expensive product than cheap one. But if the range is extended too quickly or too far from the original brand pricing, it will lack credibility and, more importantly, damage the original brand by reducing its premium perception in the eyes of all customers.

Many fashion brands have generated significant growth from extending their brands downmarket. Giorgio Armani started life as couture fashion brand. Since then it has created a succession of less expensive sub-brands to widen its appeal and increase its customer base. The brand portfolio is constantly being supported from the top by the regular bespoke fashion shows that create the richest expression of the brand. This provides a brand halo across all the other ranges and helps reinforce their desirability, even though they are mass-produced cheaper items of clothing. The Giorgio Armani brand offers luxury suits and dresses, whereas the Emporio Armani brand offers suits and more casual clothes at prices more customers can afford. Further down the portfolio, the Armani Exchange A/X brand offers products that many customers can afford. Each brand draws on the overall Armani brand image, but provides different products at different prices so as not to compete with each other. The portfolio is well-balanced in terms of revenues, with 32% coming from the Giorgio Armani brand, 27% from Emporio Armani and 14% from Armani Exchange; the rest comes from such ventures as Armani hotels and furniture. In the 2011–12 financial year, sales revenue grew by 13.6% to €1.8 billion and operating profits were €281.8m. Armani, like Ralph Lauren, has managed to create sub-brands that are appealing to more budget-conscious customers without damaging the master brand.

Once a master brand starts to lose its luxury appeal, it rapidly affects customers' perceptions and desire for the rest of the portfolio's brands. This has happened with several brands that stretched too far down the price ladder, notably Pierre Cardin.

To make a success of extending a brand downmarket, the things that marketers can do are broadly similar in principle to those that can or should be done for an extension upmarket:

- Use a clear value descriptor to help customers understand the differences in service levels and pricing between brands. For example, the more upmarket Holiday Inn (1,181 hotels worldwide) offers a full-service restaurant, whereas Holiday Inn Express (2,222 hotels worldwide) does not. Microsoft extended downwards by introducing software products with limited features, Microsoft Office Home and Business and Microsoft Office Home and Student, alongside its original Microsoft Office Professional; these products generate additional sales but at lower prices. Bang & Olufsen, an upmarket Danish electronics company, launched a new brand "B&O Play" that offers "more playful designs at more accessible price points than typically seen from Bang & Olufsen".

- Use a brand experience or packaging that signals a lower-quality, smaller product, such as cheaper materials, less printing (also often monochrome rather than full colour) or fewer components. For example, Bosch created a range of cheaper washing machines that it called Classixx and Exxcel to go with its premium Logixx range. The cheaper models have fewer electronic control features, slower spin speeds and higher noise levels than the more expensive ones. Lavazza, an Italian coffee brand, uses red packaging for its cheaper range and metallic gold packaging for its more expensive range to signal to the consumer the higher quality. Such differentiation helps set customers' expectations that the product is less valuable than the premium range.

- Choose a different sales channel, possibly online only or discount stores, to sell through. Low-cost airlines like easyJet mainly sell online with little or no telephone support and no offline retail. Aviva, a global insurance brand, sells its "Quote me happy brand" only through online channels, while its main "Aviva" brand is available through both online and offline.

- Create a clear price gap (rather than overlap) between the most expensive value product and lowest-priced premium product.

Retailing price ranges

Retailers typically use a three-tier brand portfolio strategy to sell premium, mid-priced and value ranges in their stores. This is often called the good, better and best strategy. Tesco has a "Tesco Value" range, a standard "Tesco" range and a premium range called "Tesco Finest". Each has its own distinct name, branding and packaging so that there are visible distinctions across the ranges. It helps customers choose which quality level they want for a particular product. It helps the retailer gain maximum customers by targeting their core customers with the standard range and then attracting both value and premium customers with their ranges at different prices who might have otherwise shopped at either a budget or more premium retail store. Walmart, an American multinational retailer, follows a similar sub-brand strategy with its "Sam's choice" brand for its premium offerings and "Great Value" brand for its budget products.

Mergers and acquisitions involving brands

As described earlier in this chapter, Tata has been successful at portfolio management of its Jaguar and Land Rover brands. But it also made a strategic portfolio choice to acquire the brands in the first place. In 2004 it began adding to its automotive portfolio by acquiring Daewoo Motors, a South Korean car brand, for $102m. In 2008 it launched the Tata Nano micro car targeting Indian families. In the same year it bought the Jaguar and Land Rover brands and operations for $2.3 billion from Ford, which had made money on Land Rover sales but had not managed to make a profit on Jaguar cars. Thus Tata's portfolio included the world's cheapest car, a mid-priced brand (Daewoo) and two of the world's most famous premium car brands. The portfolio logic of buying Jaguar and Land Rover is likely to have been that:

- the advanced automotive technologies and production facilities could be used across other brands;
- Tata would gain access to a new segment of premium customers that is growing rapidly in markets like India and China;
- a premium and stylish brand image might cast a halo across its other car brands;
- the gain of sophisticated brand marketing skills and experience could be used to improve the quality of the brand marketing of the other brands in the portfolio;
- it would be a new source of revenues with higher margins than Tata's value or mid-priced car brands.

The addition of the Jaguar Land Rover brands to the Tata portfolio has been a great success. In 2011, Tata increased the division's workforce by 1,000 employees. In 2012, its sales continued to grow, especially in emerging markets, with increases in the UK (3%), the United States (13%) and China (76%). In that year it sold 314,433 vehicles, more than it had done at any other time in its history, and increased profits by 37% to a record $2.3 billion. The profits generated in 2012, just four years after the brands were bought, were larger than the price Tata originally paid for the Jaguar Land Rover business.

When a company buys another brand or merges with a company that owns other brands, it can choose to:

- keep the original, pre-merger brands separate, which it will if it believes that will create most value – renaming Jaguar as Tata-Jaguar would have been a surprising decision;

- merge the brands under one, sometimes rather long name, as happened with Thomson Reuters, GlaxoSmithKline and PricewaterhouseCoopers;

- choose the name of the dominant or highest-value brand and dispense with the other, as happened when AT&T merged with SBC Communications in the belief that higher long-term value could be generated from the single AT&T brand;

- give the newly combined business a completely new name. This is rare, but when Philip Morris purchased Kraft and combined the food company with its tobacco businesses, it called the newly combined company Altria. The intention was to find a way to reconcile at the corporate level the different sectors the two companies operated in. The brands used for the tobacco and food products did not change and the Kraft business was subsequently sold.

Brand divestment

Following divestment of part of a brand business, it sometimes happens that two companies each use the same brand. This is the case with Volvo: Ford uses the brand for cars; while Volvo uses it for commercial vehicles such as trucks, construction equipment and travel coaches. Both firms meet regularly to discuss and agree brand-management policies.

The alternative is to launch a new brand. When Royal Bank of Scotland was required to divest its insurance businesses as part of the government bail-out, it chose to create and launch a new brand, Direct Line Group, prior to an IPO in 2012. This new brand was designed as a corporate master brand with a portfolio of sub-brands including

Direct Line, Churchill, Green Flag, Privilege, NIG (a B2B insurer) and Tracker (a telematics product that provides customers and insurers with data about customers' driving behaviour). As a corporate master brand, Direct Line is aimed at investors, employees and regulators, while the sub-brands are the primary customer-facing brands.

This new corporate master brand gave investors greater clarity about the total portfolio of businesses and brands and their future growth potential. It resulted in an oversubscribed IPO, especially with private investors.

Summary

Brand portfolio management is the matching of brands and sub-brands to distinct customer segments to maximise total company revenue and profit growth. The brand portfolio strategy needs to be developed through careful analysis of a company's existing brand portfolio and an understanding of customer segments, competitors' brands and market opportunities. This should result in a brand portfolio in which each component has a clear definition of its role in improving the overall brand perception and increasing sales.

Some companies, such as Samsung, operate portfolios with a single master brand for all their audiences, while others, such as Unilever, have a corporate master brand for B2B audiences and a large number of customer-facing sub-brands including Cif, Flora and Knorr. Most companies, however, have a variant on these two strategies with a dominant master brand and a couple of sub-brands; an example is BMW Group, which owns the BMW, Rolls-Royce and Mini sub-brands.

Because markets are constantly changing, it is important that companies review their brand portfolio regularly to maximise investment and return. There is money to be made in quickly exploiting new opportunities or divesting poor-performing brands. The best marketers can perform portfolio management successfully only if they are able to apply rigorous business analysis to the risks and opportunities.

8 Growth through employee engagement

WITHOUT EMPLOYEES WHO ARE ENGAGED and committed to the company's strategy, it becomes much harder for a business to grow, and there is clear evidence that firms that engage employees in a common purpose achieve higher returns overall. In their book *The Service Profit Chain*, Jim Heskett, Earl Sasser and Leonard Schlesinger demonstrate the correlation between levels of satisfaction and loyalty among employees, levels of satisfaction and loyalty among customers, and levels of profitability. As outlined in previous chapters, loyal customers are more profitable because they cost less to serve. They are also more likely to be receptive to brand extensions and to cross-selling. Furthermore, through their advocacy of the brand they bring in new customers and help strengthen the loyalty of the existing customers they communicate with. Indeed, the process that connects employee engagement, customer satisfaction and loyalty, and business growth is self-reinforcing, as Figure 8.1 illustrates.

The 2012 Towers Watson Global Workforce Study of 32,000 employees in 30 countries confirms the direct link between better-engaged employees and profits. Across all industries, firms with low employee engagement scores on average generated an operating margin of less than 10%; those with above-average engagement had a 14% operating margin; and those with "sustainable" engagement enjoyed an average operating margin of 27%. There are also many "best company to work for" league tables that evaluate the attractiveness of a firm for employees across a range of characteristics. Alex Edmans, assistant professor of finance at the Wharton School, University of Pennsylvania, assessed the companies listed on the "100 Best Companies to Work For in America" to prove the link between more

FIG 8.1 **The service profit chain**

Source: Heskett, J.L., Sasser, W. Earl Jr and Schlesinger, L.A., *The Service Profit Chain: How Leading Companies Link Profit and Growth to Loyalty, Satisfaction, and Value*

attractive firms and better stock returns. His analysis established that over the period 1984–2011 the firms on the list generated on average 3.8% higher stock returns per year than their peers.

In general, firms need to be quite structured in their approach to employee engagement. They must first attract the right kind of employees, then keep them committed with a strong employee value proposition (EVP) and a shared sense of the higher purpose of the firm so that they feel fully engaged in the business and are motivated to perform better.

Nissan, a Japanese car manufacturer, has successfully managed its 157,365 employees through its "Nissan Way" engagement programme (see Figure 8.2). This describes a way of working that is designed to bring out the best in each employee to help deliver the higher purpose of Nissan: "Enriching people's lives". The programme is used as part of new employee induction training, as continuing employee training within departments and as a guide for employees' daily behaviours. It is based on Nissan's statement that "Power comes from Inside" and is described by five "mindset" principles and five "actions".

FIG 8.2 **The Nissan way**

Nissan brand proposition: "Enriching people's lives"	
Employee proposition: "Power comes from inside" The focus is the customer, the driving force is value creation and the measurement of success is profit.	
Five Mind-sets Principles that frame our thinking	**Five Actions** Principles to guide our professional behaviour
Cross-functional, Cross-cultural: Be open and show empathy toward different views; welcome diversity.	**Motivate:** How are you energising yourself and others?
Transparent: Be clear, be simple, no vagueness and no hiding.	**Commit and target:** Are you accountable and are you stretching enough toward your potential?
Learner: Be passionate. Learn from every opportunity; create a learning company.	**Perform:** Are you fully focused on delivering results?
Frugal: Achieve maximum results with minimum resources	**Measure:** How do you assess performance?
Competitive: No complacency, focus on competition, and continuous benchmarking.	**Challenge:** How are you driving continuous and competitive progress across the company?

Source: Action guidelines for all our employees, www.nissan-global.com

These ten elements are supported by specific activities that shape Nissan's culture and influence employee behaviour. Their performance against these elements is reported annually in the company's performance scorecard and compared with previous years' scores and the long-term vision. An example of how these principles have been turned into activities is the "cross-functional, cross-cultural" mindset for encouraging diversity throughout the company. The HR team used this principle to create two career growth options for employees that encourage diversity in the workplace: the "shift career system" to help them grow in their own department; and the "open entry system" which encourages them to apply for roles outside their current department. In 2012, 230 employees applied for 164 "open" posts and 93 of them were successful. In 2009 Nissan launched an internal social-media site, N-Square, to encourage employees to share ideas and stories more widely. Some 300 online communities based on specific topics have been created and have become the focus of discussions among all regions and departments.

The programme has helped improve customer satisfaction, especially with customer service. Data on customer satisfaction from JD Power, a global market research firm, provide a measure of how well Nissan's performance has improved. The 2013 American Customer Service Index (CSI) survey of owners of cars bought between 2008 and 2012 showed that Nissan had improved its overall satisfaction score by 66 points to 797 out of 1,000 on all five criteria: service adviser, vehicle pick-up, service facility, service quality and service initiation. It also gained top three rankings in China, South Africa and Brazil. These improved employee and customer satisfaction results were been accompanied by an increase in net sales revenues of 4.9% to almost $9.2 billion between 2010 and 2012. More impressively, operating profits increased by 6.9% to $573m during the same period.

Attracting the right employees

The logic behind the link between quality of service and financial performance suggests that companies should be as scrupulous in targeting potential employees as they are in targeting potential customers. Herb Kelleher, chairman of Southwest Airlines, is credited with changing the way that many companies now select new employees. Previously, skills and experience in a particular sector were a potential recruit's most prized attributes. But his "hire for attitude, train for skills" mantra has changed how many companies assess people for jobs. For example, when Carphone Warehouse (The Phone House outside the UK) was starting out, its CEO, Charles Dunstone, was against hiring anyone who had worked for a phone retailer before, so that they would be free from preconceived ideas about customer service that did not match his company's model. In 2000 an IPO valued the company, which was launched in 1989, at around £1.6 billion. It is now Europe's largest independent phone retailer. Similarly, Larry Light, chief brand officer at InterContinental Hotels Group, believes:

In a customer-focused company, customers come second. Customer-focused employees come first; if I don't have customer-focused employees, how will I have a customer-focused business?

Aligning employees with a singular brand vision is critical to differentiation. When ING Direct launched in North America in 2000, it had a highly targeted and differentiated strategy from other banking competitors. Its aim was to strip out cost from the banking model by operating without branches and offering only simple current and savings accounts, paying higher interest rates to customers to whom its branchless model appealed. This focused customer-targeting approach was accompanied by an equally focused employee hiring method. ING's CEO, Arkadi Kuhlmann, made a point of trying not to hire people from other banks because he believed: "If you want to renew and re-energise an industry, don't hire people from that industry." The company recruited new employees who had "orange DNA" (the dominant colour of its brand identity), which was all about sharing the core values of the new company. ING encouraged its employees to put customer satisfaction first, to share a moral conviction in the value of savings and to develop an evangelical dedication to spreading this message. The effect of this was a business with more productive and loyal employees who generated greater customer value. ING Direct grew from its launch in 2000 to become one of the largest direct banks in the United States with 2,275 employees and 7.7m customer bank accounts. Just over a decade later, in 2012, the bank was sold to Capital One for $9 billion.

It takes only a little science and a lot of common sense for companies to attract the right kind of employees. A modicum of forethought and foresight in compiling interview questions reveals the best cultural fit of prospective employees. One approach is to ask a "golden question", the answer to which reveals more than might be expected. Don Peppers, founding partner of Peppers & Rogers, a management consulting firm, uses it to demonstrate the best way to find out if customers would buy premium pet food. Asking the question straight out encourages respondents to flatter themselves or try to impress the questioner. He prefers to ask: "Do you buy your pet a Christmas present?" Those who answer yes are more generous to their animals in general. A similar question for an employee might be: "What business would you start if you were given $50,000 seed capital?" There is no right or wrong answer, but it helps illuminate the attitude of potential employees.

Companies also try to see beyond the CV through the use of in-store trials for recruits. Harrah's, an American hotel and casino chain, uses a "day in the casino" test to select employees. Potential recruits work for a day in what might become their place of work. At the end of the trial, the team evaluates the recruits' performance and decides whether to hire them. Decisions are made based on how the recruits perform and get on with the team, not their previous experience and CV qualifications.

Employee value proposition

There is kudos involved in working for well-known and widely admired brands which helps underpin commitment and engagement among employees. But people do not have to work for a well-known brand to feel engaged in and proud of the work they do. Engagement depends on the EVP – why and in what way the firm is (or is not) a relevant, meaningful and satisfying place to work. A strong EVP makes a business more efficient in several ways:

- it attracts high-quality employees, which makes recruitment easier;
- employees want to be with the company and perform better;
- employees are more likely to stay with the business, which means skills and knowledge are retained and time and money spent on recruitment is reduced.

According to research by the Corporate Leadership Council on EVP effectiveness, a superior EVP can increase new employees' level of commitment from 9% to 38%, an increase of 29%, within one month of their joining a firm. This is based on a 2006 survey of 58,000 employees across 34 countries rating a firm's EVP on five criteria: rewards, opportunity, organisation, people and the work. That getting the EVP right can increase the proportion of positive advocates for a company from an average of 24% to 47% is striking given the usual mix of happy, passive and unhappy employees in most firms. An EVP is usually supported by a series of values that provide specific direction to the culture of the organisation. Zappos, an online shoes and clothing retailer now owned by Amazon, has been since it started in 1999 a quirky place to work. The Zappos Family Core Values are listed as:

- Deliver WOW through service
- Embrace and drive change
- Create fun and a little weirdness
- Be adventurous, creative, and open-minded
- Pursue growth and learning
- Build open and honest relationships with communication
- Build a positive team and family spirit
- Do more with less
- Be passionate and determined
- Be humble

Ten values may seem excessive, but there are specific linkages between happy, motivated employees and great customer service that will drive higher profitable growth. The results speak for themselves: Zappos has excellent employee satisfaction, coming 11th in *Fortune*'s "Best companies to work for" 2012 list, and 80% of employees would recommend the firm to a friend according to Glassdoor.com's 2012 employee satisfaction analysis. Zappos's customer satisfaction scores are equally good: it came second out of 617 firms tracked by the customer service scoreboard. These high levels of employee and customer satisfaction helped the company achieve annual sales of over $1 billion within its first ten years. Zappos has been owned by Amazon since 2009, but it appears to have retained its strong internal culture.

Employee engagement planning principles

The various functional departments in a business all need to work together to boost employee engagement. HR can provide understanding about human behaviour, process and performance measurement, while marketing can use its expertise in segmentation, proposition development and communication. The goal is to achieve higher performance by ensuring that employees share the same values and sense of purpose. Hand in hand with this come judgments on how to get the most out of people so that they feel stimulated while taking care to avoid overload, which will leave employees floundering amid a sense of failure. There are three guiding principles when seeking to increase employee engagement.

Focus on individuals

Organisations are difficult to change, but with the right approach individuals can be persuaded to change quite easily. Any employee engagement process should start with a segmentation of the different employee groups, such as customer-facing and non-customer-facing employees, functional areas such as IT, legal, operations and HR, and even those identified as having high management potential. A description of what the EVP is for each segment should then be drawn up with a view to discovering what changes are desirable to strengthen the EVP for that group. It may be that the group needs to have a better understanding of what the company's purpose is, and that once they do they may be keen to know what they can do differently to further that purpose. It comes down to encouraging employees' pride in their work as individuals and as part of a team. This can only be achieved through persuasion, not by diktat. The most effective way is to appeal to individuals' emotional side first, with a higher purpose or cause they can champion as described in Chapter 6.

Be practical and pragmatic

Large organisations with thousands of employees need to find simple, everyday ways to change behaviour. It is often better to take many small steps than attempt one giant stride. To begin with, progress is better than perfection. The most effective approach for large firms with tens of thousands of employees is the 70:20:10 principle. This prioritises people's activities in a pragmatic way to help everyone focus on where the time and effort should be applied:

- 70% – behaviour that is not wrong. This should be the heart of any engagement programme. It is not about introducing a sea change but about aligning and integrating what people are already doing more tightly around the single brand vision.

- 20% – making it better. Behaviour that is hurting the reputation and performance of the firm must be identified so that it can be changed. This might mean reducing the number of middle managers who are ineffective or the number of service staff on an aircraft. Careful financial analysis will reveal whether further investment will yield positive returns in a reasonable timescale.

- 10% – the new broom. Big behavioural changes should be limited to make sure that they are manageable and do not damage revenue streams.

Stress the crucial importance of the customer

All employees need to understand their role in making sure that customers are satisfied because without satisfied customers there will be no business to employ them. This is true whether they have direct contact with customers, are involved in defining and communicating the brand message, or are simply involved in making sure that some aspect of the corporate machine functions efficiently in allowing those with closer relationships with the customers to do their job. The business's target customers must be made real to employees: this can be done using words and pictures – real experiences that involve contact or observation of customers – and by asking employees to figure out which customer segment they and their family and friends or anyone else fits into. O2, a mobile phone company, has emphasised the need for employees to be customer conscious by redesigning its call-centre meeting rooms to look like its different target customer segments' living rooms. Getting closer to customers helped O2 win 2012's award from the UK Consumer Association's magazine *Which?* "Best technology services provider".

Employee engagement programmes and activities

Following the three principles outlined above will help embed the brand vision in employees' minds and also help make sure that they adapt their behaviour to align with the company's values and achieve its goals. Programmes aimed at increasing employee engagement typically have three phases, each of which will involve the following:

■ Increasing understanding – of the current context and what needs to change.

■ Mobilisation – getting managers and the people they manage ready and motivated to make the necessary changes.

■ Change – achieving the changes desired by embedding new attitudes and behaviours and ensuring commitment to the business's purpose.

The aim in getting employees to understand what needs to change, why it needs to happen now and the impact it will have on the business is to get their emotional commitment to change. Once that exists, what matters is that the actions in pursuit of change have a logic and meaning and are within the capabilities of the employees required to carry them out. In other words, the programme needs to help employees translate the company purpose and business strategy into meaningful action for them in their daily work; otherwise they may be unable to change. Recognition that people are making the effort to change is also important – in terms of praise or expressions of gratitude, providing they are perceived as genuine, or in the form of material rewards. These employee engagement programmes are typically used following a change in brand proposition or portfolio strategy to help engage employees with the new brand. The exact timing and length of each of these phases will depend on the organisation and the desired scale of change. Building on these three phases of change are four main work streams of activities.

Leadership

A 2011 study by the IABC Research Foundation found that what influenced the engagement of employees most was the behaviour of their direct managers, followed by communications with and

FIG 8.3 **An employee engagement programme framework**

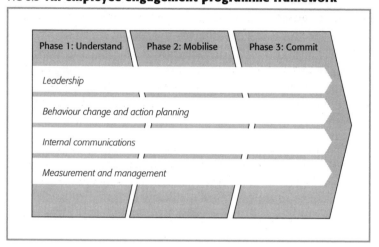

recognition of them, leadership changes and differentiated benefits. That employees are influenced by those that manage them is no surprise and demonstrates how important it is that managers behave in ways that consistently reflect the company's vision and EVP. Senior management should take responsibility for long-term actions, change and results, demonstrate their own commitment visibly and tangibly, and make sure that all managers also demonstrate their commitment. As Johann Wolfgang von Goethe said more than 200 years ago:

> *Treat people as if they were what they ought to be, and you help them become what they are capable of being.*

This thought still defines the essence of modern leadership, which is to engage and motivate others. Motivating others is often seen as a talent that some people are born with and the role of only the most outgoing individuals. But while many great leaders have great personal charisma, in her book *Quiet: The Power of Introverts in a World That Can't Stop Talking*, Susan Cain makes a strong case for the power of quiet leadership. Tony Hsieh, the founder of Zappos, also holds the view that humility is one of the most important values behind his company's success.

Encouraging new behaviour that creates growth often requires stopping or adapting previous behaviour. It is crucial that leaders demonstrate any desired new behaviour and stop behaving in ways that are no longer desired. Carlos Ghosn, the CEO who turned Nissan from a business with $17 billion of debt into one of the most profitable car brands in the world, believes that engaging employees is one of the top three prerequisites to helping a business grow, after vision and strategy:

> The biggest mistake that managers make in a turnaround is not connecting with people. You have to establish some kind of direct and indirect contact with them, you have to feel the situation, you have to understand the expectation of people and you have to respond to them, you have to respond to them in a way that is going to revive the company, that's the challenge.

Clearly he strongly believes that leaders need to engage, respond and demonstrably lead their employees through their own behaviour.

Behaviour: empowering employees

As noted earlier in this chapter, there is a strong link between employee behaviour and customer engagement, satisfaction and sales. Kenexa, an IBM HR consulting company, found that 15% of a Sainsbury's store's year-on-year growth can be explained by the level of employee engagement. This work stream involves encouraging and persuading people to align their behaviour with the company's strategy and higher purpose. It requires the identification of what new behaviours are desirable and what old ones need to be discouraged, as well as which current behaviours are acceptable.

Empowering employees to act within boundaries is in general more effective than requiring them to follow highly prescriptive rules. Rules, checklists and systems do, of course, have their place – especially where safety is an issue – but giving employees some latitude where there is no hard and fast "right" way to act is likely to engage them more in performing well. Such empowerment requires individuals to take more responsibility than they might otherwise do for the business and brand. Ritz-Carlton, for example, allows its customer-facing staff, even new recruits, to spend up to $2,000 on a guest without managerial approval, thus making it more likely that problems are resolved as quickly as possible. The policy helps convert unhappy people into brand advocates – in part because it demonstrates to guests that the company employs staff of such calibre that they can be trusted to make such decisions. For the staff, the trust and confidence placed in their judgment demonstrates that they have a direct role to play in the company's success. Overall, it ensures greater commitment to the brand. In a 2012 interview with Ashley Furness, a market analyst, Diana Oreck, vice-president of Ritz-Carlton's Global Learning and Leadership Centre, lamented the hotel industry's high staff turnover rate (60–70% a year) while at the same time celebrating Ritz-Carlton's own low rate (20%).

As employees increase their sense of empowerment, they also start to behave as "emotional owners" of the business, acting with the same duty of care, diligence and commitment that the actual owners of the business do. Companies whose employees behave in this way have a lower staff turnover, and so retain knowledge and skills and are able to build capabilities at lower cost. Furthermore, when employees feel like owners of the business they are more likely to come up with innovative ideas that help drive growth.

Employees who demonstrate these higher levels of commitment can be described as being in a state of "flow" – the mental state when a person is completely absorbed in a task and feels energised by the work involved in carrying it out. The concept was first described by Mihály Csíkszentmihályi, a Hungarian psychologist, in *Flow: The Psychology of Optimal Experience*. This state of mind is also referred to as "being in the zone".

A balance must be struck between the difficulty of a task and the capability of the individual. If the task is too easy, people will get bored; but if it is too difficult, they may become stressed and not perform well (see Figure 8.4). It is this optimising of task and capability that achieves employee excellence. In the zone, high-performing individuals (and teams) are able to maximise performance for a given task without being overcome by the stress or scale of the task. Lower-performing employees and teams fall into the rut of not being challenged enough, which is demotivating.

FIG 8.4 **Optimal experience flow diagram**

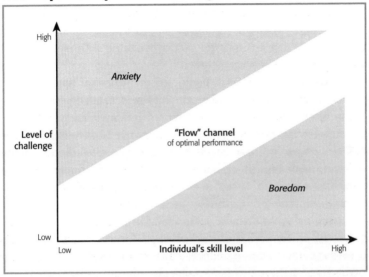

Source: Csikszentmihalyi, M., *Flow: The Psychology of Optimal Experience*

Google, which is regularly rated one of the best companies to work for, has a number of things in place that encourage "flow". Its "20% project" encourages engineers to spend 20% of their time on projects outside their normal scope that could potentially benefit the firm. It helps them explore new opportunities and strengthen their skill base, and has resulted in many significant innovations such as Gmail, Google News and AdSense. The company also has a dedicated "Google ideas" website, where ideas are rated by employees on scale of 0 to 5: 0 = dangerous; 5 = great ideas, let's go for it. It also ran an internal competition called "Project 10^100" to encourage employees to come up with world-changing ideas, and invested $10m in five winning ideas from 100 finalists to act as seeds for future business. In all, it received 150,000 innovation ideas over the three months of the competition. Openness and directness are hallmarks of organisations that create this additional employee bonding to their cause. Google uses its weekly meeting and webcast to share information and encourage discussion across the firm. The most distinct part of this is the Q&A session where employees can ask the founders or senior management any question they like about the business or their views on the future – anything is possible. Google's approach to employee ownership is part cultural and part structural. It defines the role of employees in the operating model.

Similarly, India's ICICI Bank, led by Chanda Kochhar, has restructured the role of frontline employees in its retail-banking arm. Before Kochhar became CEO, the retail bank branches were largely conduits for a strongly centralised loan business. To grow the business and strengthen its financial position, Kochhar shifted the execution of loans and deposit accounts closer to the customer through greater involvement of staff in the bank's network of branches. It required retraining thousands of employees in how to sell a loan and open a deposit account rather than just passing on information to central office. Kochar set a clear target for each large branch to open 120 new accounts per month. This gave local employees greater ownership of the part of the business they were responsible for, and customers benefited from swifter decision-making and a closer personal relationship with their bank, all of which contributed to a 54% increase in the deposit ratio in the three years following the introduction of these changes.

Internal communications

The 2011 IABC Research Foundation report identified that the second most important influencer of employee engagement was the amount of employee communications. But these communications need to clearly express the higher purpose of the firm and the EVP to be effective. Internal communications should show employees how they can realign their behaviours and the benefits of achieving this. It should also provide a mechanism to share success stories and best practices across internal communications systems such as intranets. Chapter 9 examines some of the techniques that are effective in internal communications. Repetition and reinforcement are required to make sure that all employees know where they are heading. Marketers like to change and update their messages, but greater consistency is more effective in aligning and uniting employees around a single purpose.

As in consumer marketing, internal communications should be a dialogue not an edict from senior management. AstraZeneca used a social-media intranet called Yammer to help employees engage in topics quickly and easily across countries and functions. This created a "big conversation" which quickly began to build areas of common interest within the firm, encouraging cohesion. It created a valuable platform for sharing best practice and knowledge. The self-selecting nature of social media meant that only those directly interested in a topic got involved in that conversation, thus overcoming traditional hierarchies and boundaries, and resulting in greater and more energetic commitment.

The painting of a vivid picture of the strategy can help galvanise and humanise an organisation and show what success looks and feels like. A "call to action" helps increase levels of tangible commitment from senior management and employees.

Employee engagement measures

Creating sustainable change requires supportive processes. These need to be formalised with senior management and form part of the annual review of performance measures

As noted earlier in this chapter, the level of employee engagement is a leading indicator of future customer advocacy. Companies such as Apple, Amazon, GE, Lexus and Nissan use research to link employee satisfaction, customer satisfaction and financial return. Core measures for employees should, as with marketing measures, link to the financial performance of the company, and typical measures might include the following:

- Revenue per employee – total sales divided by total number of employees. This can be important when seeking to invest in people in different parts of a business to assess different levels of employee ROI.

- Employee churn rate – number of leavers compared with number of joiners. For sectors such as the hospitality industry this can be more than 50%. This is a barrier to consistent performance and increases recruitment and training costs.

FIG 8.5 **Towers Watson: global employee engagement**
%

Highly engaged — 35
Unsupported — 22
Detached — 17
Disengaged — 26

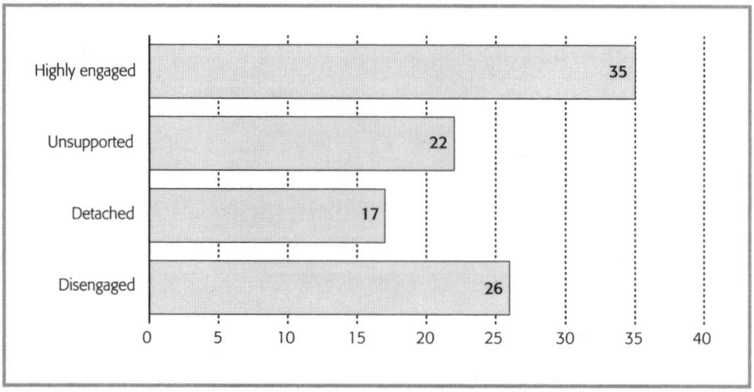

Source: Towers Watson global employee engagement survey, 2012

■ Employee engagement level – how committed employees are to the business strategy. This needs to go beyond satisfaction; happy employees are good to have but for a business to thrive it needs employees who are aligned with the aims of its strategy.

Towers Watson, a global HR consultancy, surveys hundreds of firms each year to determine levels of employee engagement. This type of external research (see Figure 8.5) enables managers to compare the results with their own research into the motivation of their workforce. As discussed in Chapter 6, companies that have a higher brand purpose generally have more motivated and engaged employees with high productivity levels.

Tony Hsieh of Zappos believes people need to bring their true personalities to work in order to be happy and productive. He rates cultural fit equally with other skills, and 50% of his company's employee performance is measured against this objective. "We want people to be the same person at home and in the office," he has stated. Employees are encouraged to create their desk as a "home away from home" with colourful decor, toys and things they value.

Summary

The more employees are engaged in their work the better they are likely to perform. Several global research studies have confirmed the statistical link between improved employee engagement and the superior commercial performance of firms. These firms benefit from creating an employee value proposition that employees can believe in and want to help deliver. That vision should provide employees with a sense of belonging and a clear set of values and behaviours that represent the firm. It is a way of doing business that is part of the competitive advantage for the firm and helps differentiate it from other firms.

Employee engagement programmes are created to motivate and educate employees about the company's higher purpose and desired employee behaviours. These programmes need to be championed if not led by the CEO if they are to succeed, and every senior manager must demonstrate the desired behaviours and not just talk about them. At the individual level, some kind of training is likely to be necessary if people are to understand the reason for change and to adapt their behaviour and attitudes accordingly. Change can take months or years to embed itself across an organisation and so it must be pursued and managed pragmatically and with clear lines of responsibility. It must also be measured and related to the business's performance.

9 Growth through customer engagement

ONE WAY TO IMPROVE PERFORMANCE is through building better relationships with customers to make their experience of the product or brand more compelling. Every contact someone has with a brand – be it an advertisement, a website, a call centre or through using a product or service – will to some extent affect their feelings towards the brand. The more positive the encounters people have with a brand the more likely they are to buy and recommend that brand in the future. The experience customers have should reflect the brand proposition (see Chapter 5) and their needs and preferences. It is one thing to take a perfect product or service to market and quite another to convince a customer to form a relationship with the brand.

The way to deepen relationships with customers is through a process of customer engagement, which involves the use of different media and the management of the entire customer experience – from making the product, having it delivered, unwrapping it and using it. For a service business, it might be researching and booking a holiday online, then travelling to the destination and enjoying the hospitality experience.

Customer engagement through media

Traditional media

Traditionally, marketing activity has been differentiated between that which is above the line (ATL) – television, cinema, billboards, radio, newspapers and magazines, etc – and that which is below the line (BTL) – direct mail, in-store promotional vouchers, etc. The main difference was whether the activity was directed at a mass audience or a narrower, targeted group of customers. Marketers generally want to create broad awareness of the brand, product or service but also to target specific promotional offers to individuals. Traditionally, the lion's share of marketing media budgets was spent on television and other ATL media. Television advertisements can be emotionally engaging for consumers with a combination of stunning visuals, catchy sound tracks and memorable words.

One of the biggest challenges of using ATL media is that it is difficult to measure its effect because it is not clear who actually viewed the advertisement and whether they purchased anything as a result of seeing it. With the increase of "on demand" television, with consumers choosing what they watch and, more importantly, when they watch it, the mass effect of television advertising is reduced, and therefore its importance as a marketing tool is less than what it was. This has decreased the effect and therefore the importance of television advertising. That is not to say that television advertising no longer has a role, but that its use as the single most important media channel is reducing.

BTL media has typically involved direct mail (these days often being in digital form rather than in print) or promotional vouchers sent to targeted individuals. Such marketing activity provides a clear incentive to purchase the product, often at a discount, and its effectiveness is much easier to measure than in the case of ATL (see customer relationship management in Chapter 2).

Paid and earned media

Marketing agencies now talk more about "paid" and "earned" media than about ATL and BTL. Paid media covers that bought directly by the company, and so includes all the ATL and BTL activities described above, as well as digital marketing activities such as paid-for display advertising – those pop-up advertisements that confront customers when they visit a website or that appear on the side of the screen during a search activity. It also includes paid-for keywords that help search engines find advertisements linked to those words so that the advertisement is ranked higher up the list of search results. For example, a broadband provider might buy the keywords "fast, download and speed" and link them to an online advertisement for its broadband product. It will also pay a search-engine company a fee if customers click through to the advertisement or its own website. Consumers might accept watching an advertising video for a few seconds before gaining access to the YouTube content they want. For example, the website of a business magazine might have a short advertising video from another product brand that plays every time a viewer logs on to it. The viewer can choose to watch or skip directly to the site, but the magazine will get paid for every customer who watches the advertiser's video fully and/or clicks through to the advertiser's website. Crucially, this type of advertising can be easily tracked to see which customers clicked on which advert, when they did it and even which web pages they looked at just before and just after they viewed the page.

Earned media is a term used to describe communications that consumers create or share with each other about a brand that is not paid for by a company. So when a consumer shares an interesting online video about Holiday Inn with friends, or writes a short blog on Facebook about staying there, or rates it on TripAdvisor, a travel-information website, Holiday Inn gains "earned media" and exposure for the brand, which, depending on what the consumer has said, may be positive or negative. The huge amount of written, picture and video-content sharing by consumers means that earned media now has a significant effect on public perception of brands. Of course, word-of-mouth recommendations from family and friends about their preferences for a particular brand have always occurred. But the use of digital media and the internet has transformed small, inter-family referrals into something that can affect a global audience, and the most popular online bloggers have become global opinion formers.

Previously, the large amount of paid-for media dominated consumers' perceptions of a brand. These perceptions are now augmented by a large amount of other people's recommendations and opinions. Research on social networks published in *Harvard Business Review* in 2011 revealed that 83% of American, British and Chinese consumers regularly recommend products and services to friends, and 84% seek a second opinion before purchasing. Increasingly, these recommendations and opinions are shared online.

FIG 9.1 **Influences and their impact on purchase decisions**

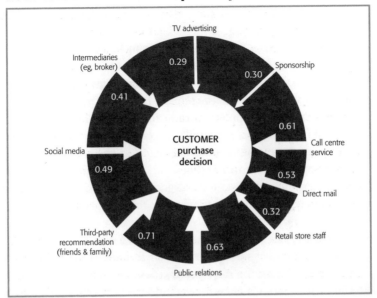

The large amount of earned media that consumers now experience creates a counterbalance to the paid-for media that companies use to influence brand purchase decisions. This creates a big challenge for marketers because consumers often perceive other consumers' opinions to be more accurate because they are independent of the company. In deciding on and planning their activities, marketers need to understand this more comprehensive picture of the influences on individuals' opinions of a brand, their buying behaviour and preferences (see Figure 9.1).

The digital transformation

Old industry adages that television advertising reaches the most people and has the biggest impact no longer hold true. Digital media and the internet now engage customers to great effect. Oreo, an American cookie brand, used this earned media to great effect during the 2012 Super Bowl football final in New Orleans. Television advertisement slots during the game are some of the most expensive in the world, costing $4m per 30-second slot. Unfortunately, there was a 35-minute power cut during the game and the TV screens went blank. The Oreo marketing team spotted a golden opportunity and seized it, sending out a Twitter tweet with a picture of an Oreo cookie with the message: "Power out? No problem. You can still dunk in the dark"; over 15,000 retweets followed and Oreo registered more than new 20,000 "likes" on its Facebook page. Because of its initial success on the night and the importance of the Super Bowl, Oreo got a huge amount of free, positive PR around the world in the following weeks.

Another example of the ability of digital media to engage global audiences virtually for free is that of a South Korean singer called Psy. His Gangnam-style dance video posted on YouTube in 2012 was watched more than 1.2 billion times in the first few weeks, prompting many video imitations. Within just a few weeks, awareness of Psy had spread around the world. The global video coverage was achieved at little cost and generated over $8m in revenues for YouTube. Its revenues come from the mini posters, paid for by companies, that appear at the beginning of each video, and YouTube gets more money when a consumer clicks through a poster to the company's website. If a company tried to buy that amount of traditional television or radio advertising, it would cost tens of millions of dollars.

These examples illustrate a number of dramatic changes that are occurring in the scope and use of media to engage customers:

■ **Scale.** A vast global audience is available through the internet for companies and individuals to communicate with each other. Such communication has benefited from the use of a shared language of the internet, English, although other languages are increasingly growing in prominence. Rapid growth in internet usage continues, with 2.7 billion internet users (39% of the global population) in 2013, according to the International Telecommunication Union's ICT Facts and Figures.

 – UN research reckoned there were 6.8 billion mobile phone users in 2012, compared with 2.2 billion in 2005. But because some of these phones are inactive and some people have more than one phone, Wireless Intelligence concludes that there were 3.2 billion unique mobile phone users worldwide in 2012. Of these, only about 40% or 1.3 billion are smartphone users able to access the internet.

- Cheap, cloud-based computing power means businesses can gain, store and access large volumes of data on customers with speed and ease, and more importantly in real time. In 2012, 2.8 zettabytes (a zettabyte is 1 billion terabytes) of data were transmitted over the internet, 48% more than in 2011. The enormous amount of content that is created every day means that people are bombarded with it, both requested and unsolicited. In 2013, every minute of every day 48 hours worth of new YouTube video content was uploaded, Facebook users shared 684,478 pieces of content and 27,778 new posts were published on Tumblr, a microblogging and social-networking website.

- **Speed.** Communications can be sent and received instantly with little or no production facilities required to prepare the content, unlike a traditional television advertisement or print campaign that might take months to prepare. For example, when Justin Beiber, a pop singer, tweets a new comment on Twitter, his 37.6m fans around the world get the message instantaneously, a task that would have taken weeks or even months to achieve before the internet. Consumers now expect to find and access information instantly wherever they are: at the office, at home or even travelling on a bus or walking down the street.

- **Ease of access.** Easy-to-use software programs and apps have made creating content and communicating it easy for everyone. The rise in use and capability of smartphones means this content can be created by individuals wherever they are. A 2013 Business Insider survey found that American consumers spend more time (144 minutes per day) using mobiles than watching TV.

- **Cost effectiveness.** One of the great attractions of the internet is how little it can cost to use. Indeed, some of the most used business and consumer channels like Facebook or Twitter are completely free with massive audience reach.

- **Person-to-person sharing.** Technological changes have resulted in profound changes in people's media use and behaviour. They now share vast amounts of personal information with others, such as holiday photos, or recommendations on products and services, such as hotels and restaurants. These large audiences are different from traditional media audiences because those who share values or interests do not need to be physically close to be targeted. It is as easy to target cat lovers all over the world as it is to target the global fan base of Tiger Woods, a golfer. These new media audiences are defined by their areas of interest not their geography. A huge amount of personal opinion is shared daily on important and trivial topics, making broadcasters out of individuals.

Marketing to people's interests

The big change that has occurred in recent years is that the internet now acts as a social network rather than just an information-sharing network, with an increasing focus on linking people and their opinions through conversations on Facebook, LinkedIn and Twitter, for example. This shift towards people-to-people social activities means that marketers need to find ways to position their brands within these social contexts and conversations to get customers' attention. Less product information and more content on customers' passions and interests will get them to "join" a brand's community of followers. Burberry's "Art of the trench" website (artofthetrench.com) encourages customers to share photos of themselves in their trench coats. The was site launched in 2009 and had 7.5m views from 150 countries in its first year. Its success encouraged Burberry in 2012 to put 60% of its total marketing budget into digital media.

Fashion may be a high-interest category, but American Express has proved that social engagement can still be achieved effectively in lower-interest categories such as small-business banking with its (www.openforum.com). This provides small-business owners access to a community of like-minded people to help them share knowledge, ideas and experiences on how to improve their business. Its "Small Business Saturday" is an online initiative that encourages people to share information about local shops and businesses and to shop locally. In 2011 President Obama and officials in 50 American states endorsed this initiative and the Senate passed a resolution to make it an "official day". American Express generated brand and business benefits from indirectly marketing to potential B2B customers and consumers. It created a topic that was so interesting and relevant that it was picked up and spread by consumers themselves, with American Express acting only as the host for the conversations or activities.

Social-media marketing

Social-media marketing is a much subtler form of customer engagement than traditional television advertising because it starts with connecting the customer's interests with brands. Pinterest, a social sharing website that lets users create pinboards of images of their favourite things, is a popular marketing tool for interior design brands such as Home Depot. The company uses Pinterest to suggest new design ideas and products that inspire customers to shop more for interior design products, ideally at Home Depot stores. Pinterest allows customers to create an online "mood board" reflecting their interests, desired products or simply images and videos that represent their personality. By 2012 Home Depot had over 13,000 followers, whose individual boards had over 8,500 followers. With 32 pinboards covering different interior design topics, Home Depot creates content for sharing with others; it also follows 280 other pinboards, building a network of pinboards.

Using interesting content helps overcome the main reason that consumers reject brands' advertising online: that it is too intrusive within their social world. For example, Home Depot avoids being too pushy by putting a range of other brands on its pinboards as well as its own-label products. So while Home Depot may be "hosting" the pinboard, its content is diverse. Providing customers with exciting ideas through social media is a highly effective way to drive them to its own website: in 2012 Home Depot's revenues from online sales were over $2 billion.

Social-media marketing is successful when the content is relevant and interesting and not overly focused on the brand or product. This increasing focus on the customer's social/business life and interests is a significant change from traditional marketing, when companies sold products mainly by talking about them and their features. Consumers are more likely to pass on or tell others about content if it is about an engaging topic rather than a commercial "sell" of a product. So in these social conversations a brand should position itself to play a supporting and not a leading role.

"Social marketing", as it is called, is an ideal way to connect like-minded people who share broad or more specialist interests. Coca-Cola has created "liquid and linked" marketing to highlight how it wants to connect its products with the socio-cultural activities or passions of people's everyday lives. It is a good example of how brands are trying to create content that is so infectious or, as Coca-Cola says, "liquid" that it is shared freely across the internet by consumers while still "linked" to its business strategy, brand and customer targets. Coca-Cola's 2012 "security cameras" videos caught the public imagination by showing acts of kindness that had been captured by the world's street security cameras. It used the content for its 2012 American Super Bowl advertisement and has since gained over 6.6m YouTube views. TED, which was established to promote "ideas worth spreading", picked the video as one of its top ten advertisements worth spreading in 2013. The video has been successful because its content is about people and life, with Coca-Cola featuring only at the end of the video. By focusing on such emotive social content, Coca-Cola hopes to increase consumer's preference and advocacy for its brand. Coca-Cola's social marketing approach helped it increase net revenues by 6% between 2011 and 2012 to $48 billion.

Social-media-based marketing is a highly cost-effective method of promoting positive experiences to hundreds of millions of people. But the same mass communication outcome can happen with unhappy customers as well. In December 2011, a FedEx customer's YouTube clip, "FedEx Guy Throwing My Computer Monitor", went viral, spreading rapidly across the internet and garnering almost 9m views. It was posted by an unhappy customer who watched in horror as his new computer monitor was literally thrown over his fence by a lazy FedEx courier. YouTube amplified the misdemeanour, and the reporting of it in every media channel from the *Huffington Post* to the *Daily Mail* caused further the damage to the brand. Matthew Thornton III, senior vice-president for American operations, publicly apologised to the customer and replaced the monitor free of charge, but the brand damage was substantial, leading FedEx to share the video internally to "remind everyone that every single package is important to you, our customers, and that actions like this are totally unacceptable".

Mutual benefits help get customers more involved

Social marketing is most effective when it is mutually beneficial or, to put it another way, something of value is exchanged between a customer and a business, just as human relationships and friendships depend on this kind of mutuality. As Dominic Grounsell, marketing director at RSA Insurance Group, confirms:

> One of the significant untapped opportunities is to use social media, particularly channels like Facebook for customer value management, engagement and retention as well as the usual customer acquisition and brand activation.

The giving, receiving and sharing of ideas, knowledge, gossip and opinions are becoming the usual ways for people to interact through the internet. This might be the emotional value of "social status" gained from inclusion in trendy Belvedere Vodka's Facebook community as much as the "recognition" value of being an officially trusted seller on eBay. This exchange of value is the critical characteristic of effective marketing for growth. Firms need to define the social benefit (beyond the functional product experience) they can provide in order to gain customers' buying preference and advocacy. Burberry customers are happy to share photographs of themselves in Burberry trench coats in the knowledge that in return they will collectively gain access to a much wider pool of photographs and fashion ideas. The more who commit, the more who benefit is the general rule. The more customers receive back from a company in rewards, the more they are willing to act on its behalf in sharing and promoting it. There is a range of exchanges from downloading a simple app or re-tweeting a comment to the more onerous task (deeper commitment) of writing a product review or hosting a support forum in exchange for exclusive content or early access to new products. This is one reason this type of social marketing is more effective in influencing wider opinions of the

FIG 9.2 **Digital engagement strategies**

Mass active sharers	Super advocates
Significant volume of advocates, may constitute nearly all customers. Low propensity to advocate unless prompted	Small but important group of individuals. High propensity to advocate driven by significant emotional involvement with brand
Low individual impact but potential for influence from entire group	Can have a significant net halo effect on customer base
Engagement behaviour often reactive, eg, submitting reviews online when prompted	Typical behaviour involves actively sharing opinion/point of view on multiple facets of product or service, even up to participation in product development

Volume
Types of advocate
Expertise

brand; customers are already willing to commit a little, to contribute something, in a way they never would with paid-for media like advertising (see Figure 9.2).

Gaining customer advocates

Marketers call customers who help promote a brand on behalf of a company "advocates". Social media dramatically increase the positive effect of that advocacy on potential customers. Brands with the highest levels of advocacy outgrow their competitors in terms of revenues by up to two-and-a-half times. Potential customers experience the advocacy of existing customers through the online comments, ratings and responses they view. The more people who like or recommend an item, the better or more popular it may be. On average, brand advocates make up 0.001% of a brand's social subscribers but are responsible for 8.4% of all brand conversations across the entire social web, according to Gartner, an IT research company. As David Still, head of brand strategy at Vodafone, confirms:

> There is an important group of "active customers" out there who have a significant influence on other consumers and the brand so it's critical we engage them in a positive dialogue.

Rating systems are a popular way to get customers to promote the brand, often scoring a product or service out of five. On TripAdvisor, potential customers can see how different types of guests – families, couples, individuals or business people – scored a hotel. Or they can see how the features of a hotel – location, sleep quality, rooms, service value or cleanliness – scored. This numeric assessment is supported by quotes from customers describing their experiences. For potential customers, the number of people scoring the hotel can help assure that the hotel is popular, while the scores themselves describe its quality. For the hotel, this type of mass advocacy is helpful in providing a general consumer opinion, which is more revealing than the official or travel-industry star ratings.

Many firms now use e-mail and text messaging to encourage customers to score them following a purchase. For example, Symantec, a software security company, sends an e-mail to everyone who purchases its Norton anti-virus software asking them to rate the product in order to increase the number of ratings. These ratings will appear on Symantec's website and other computer-related websites that review this type of software, increasing the likelihood that Norton will be perceived as both excellent and popular. This will strengthen potential customers' trust that Norton is the right choice. The level of engagement between the brand and these types of advocates is low, often requiring prompts or future discounts from the company. Individual customer ratings might have little or no influence, but large numbers of them can have a strong influence on potential customers. These types of social-media activities have helped Symantec's continued financial growth, with a year-on-year increase of 10.1% in revenues in 2012 to $6.73 billion at an operating profit of 25.2%.

Gaining expert advocates

Marketers can also target a second, smaller set of advocates that have much greater influence: the experts who are recognised as frequent users and/or as having deep product knowledge that can be trusted. Experts are often willing to invest much free time and energy in reviewing or blogging about products – and may be happy to create lengthy opinion blogs or frequently update their blogs and even participate in free product-development activities for a company. For example, Norton's anti-virus software was rated "Editor's choice 2013" by *PC Magazine*. The expert reviewers analysed a range of competitors and confirmed that Norton was one of the top three performers out of 40 similar brands. The combination of high customer advocate volumes and ratings as well as expert ratings helps make sure that Norton is more appealing to prospects. Microsoft has a strong, independent expert advocate known as Mr Excel (www.mrexcel. com). On some days, his website gets more visits than Microsoft's own Excel page. Mr Excel acts as a vocal advocate and an expert instructor, helping users identify the best way to use the product and solve their technical problems. In return, Microsoft supports Mr Excel's efforts with insider knowledge on the product and previews of new releases. Products that are new to the market, technically advanced or complex, such as mortgages or pensions, often benefit more from expert advocates than from large numbers of consumer advocates.

The bonds of loyalty

Loyal customers, as outlined in Chapter 1, are what every business wants because they usually buy more, cost less to serve and are more likely to act as advocates for the brand. Some strong service brands, such as First Direct, a UK telephone and internet bank, and Amazon, develop considerable attitudinal loyalty among their customers because of their focus on customer service. Other brands use loyalty programmes to build a strong relationship with their customers, encouraging them to continue buying because they gain additional benefits for doing so – and the more they expect to be rewarded. As well as encouraging customers to buy more or more often, loyalty programmes have a number of commercial uses. For example, they can:

■ Provide valuable customer purchase behaviour data that allows firms to tailor product ranges better and target individual customers with offers likely to appeal to them.

■ Keep a brand on par with the competition. There are three main airline loyalty partnerships that recognise their own members' loyalty schemes – Star Alliance, Oneworld and Sky Team. These networks aim to lock customers into a specific group of collaborating airlines to retain revenues. All three were founded within four years of each other, 1997, 1999 and 2000, respectively, to help keep their share of travellers.

■ Present an additional marketing and social-media presence. Tasti D-lite, a New York-based company, rewards customers not just for buying its frozen desserts and drinks but also for increased social-media advocacy. Its "Treatcards" loyalty scheme offers customer double points if they link their Twitter and Foursquare (a location-based social network that lets friends know which bars and restaurants you are in via your mobile phone) accounts to the loyalty scheme. When a customer buys a product or redeems a reward, their Twitter and Foursquare accounts automatically send a tweet about it or post their location on Foursquare. The customer gets greater rewards without any extra effort in return for positive social-media activity. In 2012, one in five Treatcard members were generating traffic on more than one social network and 18% of Treatcard members were generating automatic check-ins on Foursquare.

Loyalty programmes are sometimes limited to just a single brand. Subway, a sandwich store franchise, offers a "Subway" card, which can be credited with money for buying sandwiches and used to store reward points and access discount offers. Other programmes such as Airmiles or the UK Nectar card allow customers to pool the points they earn from buying from many different partner brands and then "spend" on benefits from any of the partner brands. Successful loyalty programmes help service businesses build customer commitment to the brand on the basis of rewarding customers according to the level of their loyalty to the brand.

Mobile marketing opportunities

The rise in smartphone and tablet use is increasing the amount of social networking and contact between brands and customers and customers themselves. Smartphones have changed the way people shop, with over 95% of smartphone owners in the UK having researched a product or service on their device. Mobile-enabled social media allow customers to check offers and reviews before, during and after purchase. For example, in the pre-Thanksgiving week in the United States in 2012 there was a 50% increase in "offer e-mails" opened on a mobile phone or tablet; an estimated 27% of smartphone owners consulted reviews before making purchases; and 55% used their mobile devices to check prices while in a store. The use of apps or software applications has become a primary way for brands to engage customers because they are easy to use for answering questions as well as for entertainment and information sharing.

As accessing online content via a mobile phone or tablet becomes more common, marketing will need to be time and location specific to be effective. For example, electronic discount vouchers can be tweeted, texted or e-mailed to customers while they wait at the train station in the morning, but deliberately not while they are at home in the evening where the voucher is unlikely to be used. Average UK users now spend over two hours a day on their mobile phone or tablet, with 81% of that time dedicated to using apps. Similarly, in the United States, the average tablet and smartphone user now spends 94 minutes per day using apps. The number of apps downloaded per year is forecast to grow from 45 billion in 2012 to 310 billion in 2016.

Mobile payments (using a smartphone as a wallet) are expected to grow hugely, with $17 billion worth of mobile payments forecast to be made globally in 2013, compared with $141m in 2011. Michael Gowar, senior manager for mobile at Visa, predicts that by 2020 over 50% of all Visa transactions globally will be made using a mobile phone. The challenge for brands, retailers and customers is that there are many competing platforms to work with, including online payment systems such as PayPal, banking apps such as Barclaycard's Pingit and mobile phone providers' programmes such as Japan's NTT DOCOMO, which had 35m registered users of its mobile wallet in 2012. L2, a digital innovation think-tank, forecast that the true growth market for retailers is m-commerce, as more than 20% of e-sales in the UK are expected to be completed using mobile phones or tablets in 2013.

Engagement through experience

Many things can influence a customer's choice before purchase, but actual experience of a product or service will affect their impression of

FIG 9.3 **Starbucks: core customer experience elements**

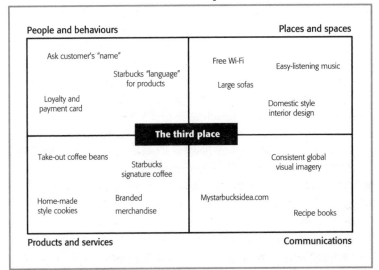

the brand. The most successful brands manage to provide customers with experiences that are distinct and consistent time after time. For example, Singapore Airlines offers its first-class travellers individual mini-cabins rather than just a seat on its A380 long-haul aircraft. BMW has created a unique iDrive computer system that tailors the controls of a car to suit a driver's needs. These distinctive brand experiences can also be about convenience and simplicity, for example a "one-click" shopping feature that allows customers to purchase things without entering their banking and delivery details every time they make a purchase. Or they may involve the personal touch – for example, writing a customer's name on the cup, as Starbucks does, to express the brand proposition through the four main elements of the customer experience: people and behaviours; places and spaces; products and services; and communications (see Figure 9.3). Starbucks describes its brand and experience thus: "We're not just passionate purveyors of coffee, but everything else that goes with a full and rewarding coffeehouse experience, a neighbourhood gathering place, a part of the daily routine."

A visit to any Starbucks cafe shows how this brand proposition has been built into each of the four aspects of the total customer experience and could be described as follows:

- **People and behaviours.** Employees are lively and gregarious, creating a welcoming atmosphere; customers can stay as long as they like, whether they order a meal or a single cup of coffee.

- **Places and spaces.** The interior design is relaxed with soft, oversized sofas, domestic lighting, music and colourful wallpaper. This contributes to the feeling of well-being, making it a comfortable place to linger. Contrast this with the utilitarian look and feel of McDonald's restaurants.

- **Products and services.** The food has a homely "comfort" style with large, misshapen cookies and lots of sugary treats. Free Wi-Fi is standard.

- **Communications.** Employees ask customers their names when they order and write them on each paper cup. This is intended to increase the sense of friendliness and make sure that the right person gets the right coffee.

Howard Schultz, chairman and CEO of Starbucks, is convinced about the importance of the customer experience. He opened the company's 2012 annual general meeting by asking Starbucks shareholders to stand and recognise the company's 200,000 partners (employees) around the world who deliver the "Starbucks experience" to customers each day – and who helped the company to achieve a 14% increase in revenues in 2012 compared with 2011.

Hallmarks of distinction

Not every part of the customer experience needs to be truly distinctive because the customer is often not willing to pay for that difference. In their minds customers trade off things that are really important to them about a product and the price they are willing to pay for it. For example, young mobile phone users might be happy to pay extra for a larger screen but are less willing to pay for product insurance or longer battery life. Marketers use research and insights to define what the most important parts of the customer experience are and then invest in making these as distinctive as possible, while endeavouring to make sure that the rest of the experience is as good as it is with competitors. Marketers call these important and distinctive parts of the customer experience branded hallmarks, which strongly embody the brand proposition and help customers' differentiate the brand from the competition. Branded hallmarks act as a tangible example of the brand proposition and are often trademarked. In 2013 Apple got an American trademark for the unique design of its stores, with long wooden tables and clear glass fronts. Examples of successful branded hallmarks are:

- Amazon's "one-click" shopping checkout (now much adopted by others)
- Hyundai's industry-beating ten-year/100,000-mile power train warranty
- Dove's campaign for real beauty and the use of real customers in its adverts
- Mercedes Benz's foot-operated handbrake

The best brand hallmarks are compelling and easy to communicate, and embody a clear customer benefit and the brand attributes in a tangible experience (see Figure 9.4).

Nordstrom, a clothing retailer, has made customer service its hallmark and in the process has demonstrated that customers will pay a higher price for a superior service. The underlying philosophy is that at all times the most important person in the business is the customer, and to make sure that this is a reality employees are well-trained and given an employee manual that says: "Use your good judgment in all situations. There are no additional rules." It is this simplicity and empowerment of employees to "go the extra mile" that defines the Nordstrom service hallmark and there are many stories of how it operates: one is of a store accepting the return of a product that Nordstrom never sold; another is of an employee teaching someone to tie a bow tie because there wasn't a clip-on one in stock. Nordstrom's growth in earnings before interest and tax (EBIT) from $779m in 2008 to $1.3 billion in 2012 is clear evidence that this kind of hallmark service makes a big difference.

FIG 9.4 **Three components of successful hallmarks**

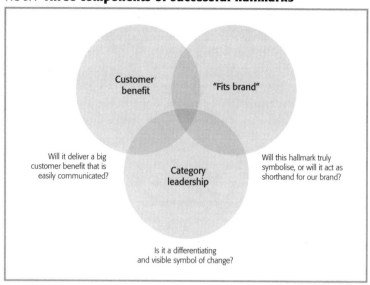

Will it deliver a big customer benefit that is easily communicated?

Customer benefit

"Fits brand"

Will this hallmark truly symbolise, or will it act as shorthand for our brand?

Category leadership

Is it a differentiating and visible symbol of change?

Improving the experience

There is a lot involved in managing the customer experience so that it is as good as it needs to be. Every employee has either a direct or an indirect influence on the customer's experience of the brand and, like an orchestra, they must all work in harmony. A five-step process can help make sure that they do (see Figure 9.5).

Diagnosis and analysis

Once there has been a diagnosis of which marketing media and parts of the customer experience have the most effect on a specific customer segment and their likelihood to purchase, there can be an analysis of the current performance of the brand against them. A media effectiveness evaluation can be carried out using many of the techniques described in Chapter 2. This should compare how much is spent on each media channel and the financial returns that resulted from that spend. This gives a clear picture of how closely the current spend is aligned with the business growth strategy. It is important to analyse media channels separately and in combination as some work

FIG 9.5 **Marketing and customer experience improvement process**

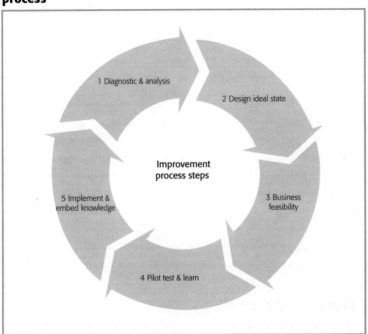

more effectively together. A quantitative analysis of individual parts of the customer experience, often called touch points, helps identify the statistical links between customers' satisfaction with different bits of their experience and their overall satisfaction with the brand. This satisfaction score can then be linked to customer value. The scores can be ranked to identify which are the most important components of overall satisfaction. Typically, just a few of these touch points will account for most of it (see Figure 9.6).

Customer expectations often change when market innovations happen. For example, in the travel-industry websites played a minor role; but with the growth of online booking and sites like expedia.com and lastminute.com, the website touch point has transformed the sector and resulted in few travel firms having much in the way of a physical presence.

FIG 9.6 **Customer satisfaction components**

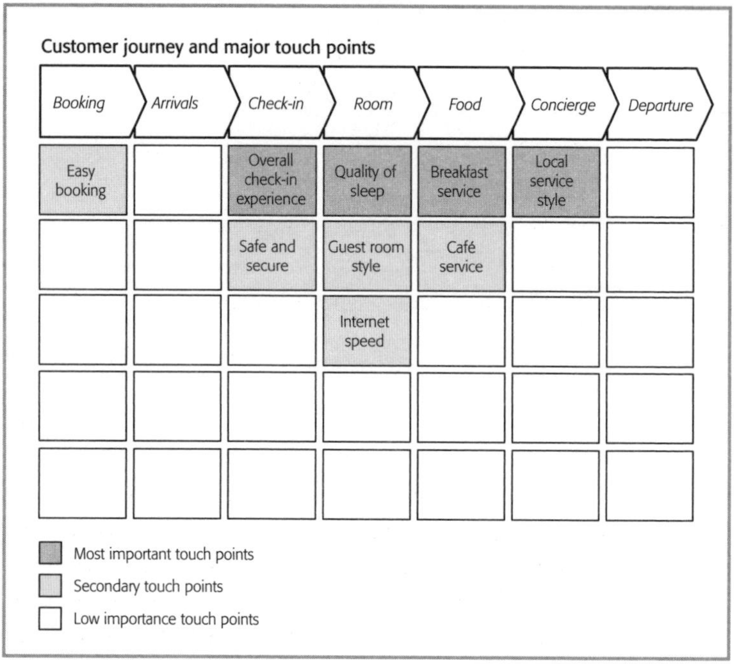

Customer journey and major touch points							
Booking	Arrivals	Check-in	Room	Food	Concierge	Departure	
Easy booking		Overall check-in experience	Quality of sleep	Breakfast service	Local service style		
		Safe and secure	Guest room style	Café service			
			Internet speed				

Most important touch points

Secondary touch points

Low importance touch points

Design

The second phase involves designing the ideal customer experience, taking care to harmonise the media experience with the product experience. There are four main components of the design process, as described earlier in this chapter, covering the product or service; people and behaviours; channel and environment; and communications.

Commercial feasibility

This is the process of making sure that what it takes to deliver the experience is justified by the financial returns and risk involved (see Chapter 2 for the techniques used). Apple's investment in creating in its retail stores a genuinely differentiating touch point that heightens the customer experience has clearly paid off. In August 2012 Apple stores were the most productive in America, generating annual revenues of $6,123 per square foot, whereas the largest pharmacy chain, CVS, with over 7,000 stores, managed only $676 per square foot, according to RetailSails, a research and consulting firm.

The investment analysis should include:

- business, customer and brand benefits;
- costs, including development, capital expenditure (capex) and operating;
- potential risk to the business and potential customer defection if they do not like the change;
- potential for short-term gains from the investment.

Different companies will have different criteria for each of the above but they form a good checklist.

Digital marketing media investment

For many businesses, media spend accounts for the largest proportion of the marketing budget, and with the shift to digital it has become even more important to make sure that marketing resources are allocated wisely. Ford used cost-effective digital media rather than traditional (and expensive) television advertising to promote the launch of the popular Fiesta car in North America in 2010. It gave 100 free cars to highly influential social-media users so that they could share their experience and views with their followers. A campaign that cost only $5m (a sum that might have bought around five 30-second evening TV slots) resulted in 6.5m YouTube views, 50,000 requests for information about the car (almost exclusively from non-Ford owners) and sales of 10,000 cars in the first six days. As a result of the campaign, Ford reallocated its investment in social media from 18% of its total media budget in 2008 to 25% in 2011.

This is not just true for consumer marketing activities in digital media; it can be cost effective for B2B marketing as well. The chief marketing officer of Fidelity, a financial services firm, has dramatically shifted the focus of the marketing spend in recent years. Social media now account for around 40% of the marketing budget. Fidelity uses social media to market its investment and equity funds, reaching both B2C and B2B customers and prospects through targeting online communities that are interested in investments (see Figure 9.7).

FIG 9.7 **Fidelity: marketing budget changes, 2008 and 2011**

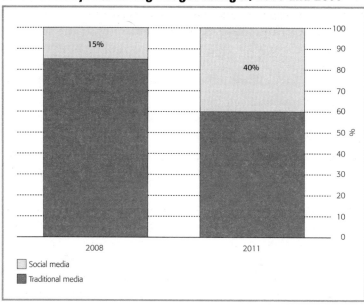

Source: www.cmo.com, "Fidelity Investments marketing leads with digital", September, 2012

Digital channels and social media present a great opportunity to engage customers by involving independent outsiders whose views will carry more weight than what a company says about its own products and services. The key to success is to work out what makes online content stand out, entertain and be of use to the customer.

Piloting

Pilot testing should be used to help refine the customer experience. This means that the pilot site, store, product or service should be used to prototype the desired new customer experience and refine the design based on customer and employee feedback. The feedback should be used to adjust the design until it fulfils the brand proposition. Test and learn, or "A-B" testing, is a way of checking which changes have the most impact against a control version where no changes are made in a live market. It is useful for large corporations to test ideas on a small scale because of the limited investment and smaller risks. The new customer experience can be tested in one market and the results compared over time with those from another market, the "control", where no changes were made to the touch point design. The results from both markets can be compared to identify improvements in revenues. No consumer test is ever perfect, but it will provide helpful and possibly invaluable insights.

Implementation

Implementation plans must cover what needs to be done, when and by whom – and it must be clear who is responsible overall (that is, who owns the project). Making sure that any new knowledge about the customer is captured and communicated within the organisation will help in improving the customer experience still further. The first step in transferring that knowledge across the organisation is training sessions with marketers and those who have contact with customers that focus on how the new customer experience matches any new insights into customers and their needs, and how it might be enhanced to produce greater financial rewards. A systematic approach is the best way to make sure that marketing activity is organised to improve customer acquisition and retention rates.

Summary

Increasing customer engagement and improving the customer experience make it more likely that a business will attract and retain customers and be able to increase the revenues it gets from them. The trick is to emotionally engage customers in ways that are relevant and valuable to them. The effect of traditional paid-for media channels such as television advertising is being counterbalanced by an equally influential range of digital-media channels that companies have much less control of. This requires marketers to connect a much wider range of direct and indirect influences on customers' buying decisions. Because customers have much greater access to and control of digital-media channels such as Facebook and Twitter, marketing needs to change its approach from one of direct "control" to one of influence, engagement, listening and working with customers to achieve results.

But there are great benefits in engaging customers to become more loyal and act as free promoters of a brand and its products. Loyalty programmes that offer customers additional benefits in rewards for extra purchases help increase revenues and profits. Increasingly, these loyalty schemes are also being used to reward customers for promoting the brand through social media in return for those rewards and discounts. Successful brands use the customer experience to reinforce brand differentiation. They use brand hallmark experiences at a few distinctive points to satisfy customers, encouraging them to be more loyal. This is much more cost effective than spreading marketing resources thinly across every aspect of the customer experience. By adopting a systematic approach to customer experience design, marketers can increase the growth of and return on their investment.

10 Growing service-based brands

SERVICES NOW ACCOUNT FOR 80% of GDP in the United States and the UK and over half of economic output for eastern European countries and some emerging economies such as India. This chapter describes the specific marketing techniques (in addition to those described in earlier chapters) that can be used to improve the performance of a service business (concentrating on the service as opposed to product element that is involved in, for example, pensions or other investments sold by financial services companies).

Process

It is the interactions of those working for a business and the business's customers that to a large extent determine the quality of the customer experience, and so the process through which those interactions take place needs to be designed to meet the customer's needs and be as efficient as possible. It needs to take into account what the "back office" must do to support what those on the "front line" are saying to and doing for customers. And it is not that simple, as the example in Figure 10.1 illustrates.

Figure 10.1 highlights the difficulties for all service businesses. The activities of those behind the scenes have to be aligned with the activities of those on the front line in order to achieve a level of service that can be repeated every day. The number of people and processes involved makes that hard to achieve. It is therefore crucial to concentrate on what the customer wants – and to design the process to suit the preferred target customer. This means being clear about the relative importance of different service elements to the customer; for

FIG 10.1 **Restaurant service processes overview**

Customer processes	Frontline employee processes	Back-office processes
■ Book online for an evening meal ■ Be greeted and seated by the restaurant manager ■ Order food and drinks from waiter ■ Food arrives and eat ■ Plates cleared away by waiter ■ Receive bill ■ Pay and receive a receipt ■ Escorted out and retrieve coats	■ Kitchen staff buy fresh ingredients and prepare them during the day ■ Restaurant cleaned and tables set ■ Staff put on uniforms and take reservations ■ Greet and seat customers as they arrive ■ Waiters take food orders and relay to the kitchen ■ Kitchen staff cook the prepared ingredients for the chosen meal ■ Waiters deliver food to the customers ■ Following the meal, the waiter presents the bill, takes the money and issues a receipt ■ Waiter escorts customers out ■ Kitchen staff clean the plates and kitchen	■ HR hiring and management ■ IT management ■ Operational management ■ Ordering goods and services ■ Financial management ■ Food hygiene and safety management

example, how much does the target customer care about being given advice on choosing wine?

The aim should be to create memorable experiences. These are often the hallmarks of a great service brand, as discussed in Chapter 9. For example, L.L. Bean, an American clothing retailer, has a "Going the extra mile-lifetime guarantee" and offers to replace products "at any time" if they deliver less than 100% satisfaction. Sales staff simply mark the returned goods as defective and give the customer a new product. The way in which staff accept the returned product without argument or trying to avoid replacement demonstrates their commitment to customer service. Volkswagen invites customers to pick up their new car from its Autostadt site in Germany. They can stay overnight for free and then watch as a hydraulic lift selects their car from a glass tower block containing hundreds of new VW cars, and are then shown how the car's features work before leaving. It all adds up to a truly memorable customer service experience. Progressive Casualty Insurance Company in the United States uses an "immediate response" team of mobile insurance assessors who can quickly reach an accident site, assess the damage and often pay the necessary costs on the spot. This cuts costs in several ways; it reduces legal fees, bureaucracy and fraud while making customers delighted to have everything resolved so quickly.

Marketing helps set consumer expectations by communicating what the service experience is like. This might include the level of service, from full service to self-service. For example, a TV advertisement for a theme park such as Disney World describes the level of service and entertainment that customers can expect; or the design of a McDonald's restaurant helps to communicate that the experience is self-service, simple and no frills.

Demand-service experiences must be created when and where the customers want them. A role of the marketing function is to develop an understanding of customer behaviour in order to forecast peaks in service demand – and ideally to manage and shape demand. For example, Avis has to balance the rental of its cars to maximise rented-out time and minimise unrented time. Avis has over 500,000 cars that it rents out at over 10,000 locations, which means (ignoring days cars are off the road for repairs and servicing) it can sell up to 182.5m car rental days to customers a year. It achieved 125m rental days in 2012, generating revenues of over $7 billion, which implies that for every 5m additional rental days it might have sold it would have increased its revenues by $280m. Maximising service "up time" not only brings in more revenue but also, more importantly, disproportionately increases overall profitability because staff and other overhead costs are largely fixed, regardless of how much the business's cars – its assets – are rented out.

Data analysis of customer rental patterns can identify peaks in demand, location and low usage times throughout the year, which helps Avis increase its overall rental time and profitability. Through marketing, it should be possible to persuade customers to rent vehicles in a slightly different pattern that helps smooth out those peaks and troughs in demand and make the business more efficient. Ways of managing demand include the use of marketing promotions to make non-peak times more attractive to customers. A typical technique is to offer customers better deals on mid-week rentals when fewer people normally book or during the winter when fewer people go on holiday. Marketers can also use non-price-driven offers such as upgrades for the same price for those willing to change their travel dates or times slightly. Customers understand the give and take of gaining rewards for themselves in exchange for helping the company manage demand for its service. Businesses are becoming increasingly more explicit about the customer benefits in trade-offs that will help the company.

Price

The price someone is willing to pay for a service can vary substantially according to circumstances that affect demand. For example, people may be willing to pay more for flying on a specific date or they may be happy to be flexible if it means saving some money; or they may be willing to pay more for a mobile phone service that guarantees faster downloads. Businesses generally try to get as much of their service capacity allocated (sold) in advance. They generally have to pay to run those services whether customers buy them or not, and if they "sell out" they may have the ability to add capacity. Marketers can use their knowledge of customer behaviour to help define which times of the day, week or year are more valuable to different segments and adjust prices accordingly.

The management of price and timing of demand is often called yield management. Ryanair, a European budget airline, has become expert at juggling its prices to fill its planes and it enjoys the highest load factor in the industry (see Figure 10.2). It is now Europe's second largest airline, carrying 79.6m passengers in 2012 when profits were a record £460m. Ryanair was one of the first airlines to quote only the basic price of the flight, with additional charges for things like checked-in bags and manual (as opposed to online) check-in being made clear only when people were in the process of booking.

People

Hiring the right people and then getting the best out of them is particularly important for a service business. Chapter 8 covers the tools and techniques used to engage employees but that is only one of the elements involved in making sure that the attitude and resilience of those on the front line provide a consistent customer experience however they may be feeling themselves at any particular time.

FIG 10.2 **Major airlines' seat occupancy figures**

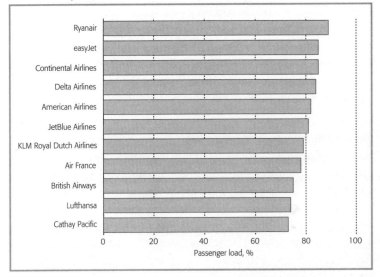

Source: www.centreforaviation.com, 2013

Managing expectations

The main reasons that service businesses fail to satisfy customers is that customers' expectations of the service are too high or too varied. One customer may be happy to select from different options from an online car insurance brand; others may expect to be guided through the different options available. The problem of varied expectations can be addressed as follows:

■ Being flexible enough to accommodate customers' wide-ranging needs. Added-value businesses like law and wealth-management firms and upmarket hotels favour this approach. The clients of lawyers and wealth managers have a unique combination of goals and personal circumstances and professional advisers are accustomed to providing a personalised service. Similarly, top-of-the-range hotels are used to dealing with extraordinary requests from some of their customers.

■ Limiting customers' options. Businesses such as McDonald's and Ryanair at the budget end of a sector do this. But so do premium

businesses such as Eurostar, which offers its customers a fixed
network of rail routes and only three classes of seats – standard,
standard premier and business premier – which gives it little
room for personal tailoring. At the luxury end of the market,
limited choice can be a hallmark of the brand – attracting people
who want the best and who accept that the brand knows best;
hence the limited-choice menus in some top-class restaurants.

Freedom within a framework

There is often a balance to be struck between efficiency and consistency
when tailoring a service to customers' individual tastes. Many people
will pay a premium for a service that is both familiar but also slightly
tailored to their needs. Starbucks has a fixed set of coffee-bean
flavours (Java, Kenya, etc) and a few different ways of making coffee
(cappuccino, espresso, etc), but it allows customers to adapt these
combinations to suit their own tastes. So a customer might order a
Java cappuccino with an extra shot of coffee and a vanilla flavouring.
This gives customers a feeling of personalisation that they value. But
the company also retains the benefit of standardisation in two ways.
First, the vast majority of customers will choose the standard coffee
bean with a couple of ways of making it and a couple of sizes, so the
average range of different drinks required may be less than ten for 80%
of customers. Second, the small number of customers that tailor their
drinks are doing so from a limited set of readily available components
that take little or no extra time to produce. The challenge is to initially
gauge and then refine the optimal balance between process efficiency
and individual personalisation that will maximise profits.

Automated benefits

The quality of customer service can be hugely enhanced by cleverly
designed automated services that add value and make customers' lives
easier. When Amazon introduced its one-click shopping checkout in 1997
it saved customers having to input their personal details whenever they
made purchases through the site. In 1999 it got an American patent for
"one-click" and since then the term has become ubiquitous for easy buying
online. So much so that in 2000 Apple licensed the one-click feature from

Amazon for its own online store, and many other companies have set up systems that make the online checkout process simpler and quicker. The ease of one-click shopping has undoubtedly contributed to the amount of retail business done online. Amazon has also sought to make life easier for its customers by tracking their purchases and what they have looked at on the site to come up with personalised recommendations of books, films, music, and so on for each customer.

Involving the customer

Self-service has spread to supermarket checkouts, airline check-in and all kinds of online activities. Many people now manage their bank accounts online, making payments and transfers whenever they like. This increases convenience to customers and saves banks substantial amounts of money in terms of the number of branches and staff they need. Depending on their abilities, customers have the power to make the service better, worse, faster or slower through their own actions. Some businesses, such as gyms, social-media sites or online dating services, require a high level of consumer involvement, without which the service would not be "completed". Others, such as fast-food restaurants or airlines, require minimal involvement from the consumer; employees do everything else.

The more dependent a business is on consumer participation, the more important it is to "train" and manage consumers effectively in order that both parties to the transaction benefit. Customers must first understand what their role is in the service delivery. For example, airline customers play a minor role, mostly having to turn up, sit down and be served; conversely, online dating service customers play a major role, searching for potential partners on a website, conversing with and getting to know them, and setting up and going on dates. Marketing can help communicate what is expected from customers – and how they need to act to get the most out of the service. As Frances Frei, UPS Foundation Professor of Service Management at Harvard Business School, recommends: "The service and consumer's specific involvement needs to be designed to deliver outstanding results with only average customers." This might seem like a low target, but if the target is for superhuman consumers, the majority of average consumers will experience a poor result.

One successful example of a service brand that has helped train customers' behaviour is PruHealth, a private health insurer which is part of Prudential, a global insurance firm. It has created a "vitality points" scheme to complement its personal health insurance, helping its customers to live more healthily. New customers take part in an online induction showing them how taking care of their mind and body will result in cash rewards at the end of each year. The amount received ($150–500) depends on how actively they look after themselves. There are online training modules and offline partner discounts to help customers improve their health by losing weight, stopping smoking, eating more healthily and reducing stress. Vitality points are awarded for increased participation in each of these activities, which are converted into cash at the end of each year. By training its customers to be healthier, PruHealth benefits from fewer claims and increases its profitability; customers benefit from being healthier and gain cash as well.

Using customers to help with service delivery also helps grow a service business. Because service businesses require staff, it can be difficult to achieve rapid growth and maintain quality. One of the most effective win-win service designs using customers' efforts is eBay's "rate seller and buyer" evaluation system. The company's business model relies on people's "trusted seller and/or buyer" status to survive because without it people would be reluctant to hand over cash or products to strangers. With millions of buyers and sellers, it would be enormously costly for eBay to evaluate and rate each person and sales transaction itself. It would make the service unaffordable to most people. By using the eBay community to self-score transactions, buyers and sellers, eBay has saved money and provided users with peer reviews that increase the sense of community and commitment. Both eBay and buyers and sellers benefit from the system; eBay keeps costs low and those savings are passed on to customers. Founded in 1995, it now has over 112m active users and more than 350m listings globally. Its revenues grew by 15.4% between 2011 and 2012 to $14 billion, with its EBITDA reaching $4.75 billion.

Some businesses are even getting customers to take over the training and troubleshooting of problems for other customers. Giffgaff, a mobile phone operator owned by Telefónica, a Spanish telecommunications company, offers lower-priced tariffs than competitors to customers who are willing to provide help to other customers in return for rewards and lower prices. Giffgaff "members" can create "help" videos that solve or explain typical phone or network problems, answer queries and promote the brand in return for cash, call credits or charity donations. Since 2010, Giffgaff members have answered over 8,000 customer queries and the response time is about 3 minutes (the industry average is 15 minutes). Some members have earned around $1,500 in discounts rewards.

Exclusive appeal, extra margin

One of the most effective ways to generate higher profits is to encourage customers to buy higher levels of services for which you can charge much more than the additional cost over the basic or standard level. Creating a ladder or range of services such as gold, silver and bronze means that:

- a broader set of customers can purchase the service or product through staggered pricing aimed at different customer segments, each with its own perceived and actual benefits, yet with economies of scale that result in an increased overall margin – for example, the fixed costs, such as fuel, of running a scheduled flight service are the same but some passengers pay much more than others to fly business, premium or first class;

- customers can purchase multiple offers to match different needs or occasions – for example, when buying tickets from British Airways online, customers are offered hotel, car rental and sightseeing deals for the destination that can be booked at discounted rates with partner brands such as Avis;

- customers can be tempted to try something out and later be persuaded to upgrade – for example, with a satellite or cable TV service, it is common for people to initially subscribe to a basic package of channels and later add other options such as film or sports channels.

American Express has developed a portfolio of credit cards from its original green charge card. These are designed to appeal to different needs but there is still a hierarchy, from the Basic card through the American Express card, the Preferred Rewards Gold card, the desirable Platinum card and the largely unattainable Centurion card, which the company describes as: "Rarely seen, always recognised." It is an invitation-only card that offers holders a "level of service that can be extended only to selected individuals worldwide". The psychology of credit cards follows two rules of importance: first, what is at the front of a customer's wallet; and second, what colour it is. This visible pecking order can create a dissonance among customers who wish to demonstrate their financial status through a "badge of honour". This dissonance encourages exclusivity and desirability as customers try to advance up through the tiers, engendering greater loyalty as they progress. A flash of platinum or black in the wallet is highly sought after. Maintaining a clear distinction between the service tiers is crucial for this strategy to work.

Summary

Managing and marketing services require different techniques from product marketing because they are intangible, often time-based and usually involve interaction with frontline service employees. This increases the variability and unpredictability of customer purchasing behaviour and makes it more important that the customer service experience is consistently good and appropriate. Service brands must combine efficiency with consistency but it helps if they also have the ability to offer customers some personalisation of the service. Introducing an element of self-service or customer involvement is a good way of reducing costs as well as providing personalisation. Customers might receive additional benefits as a reward for the part they play or the work they do in serving themselves – perhaps special access to online content or a discount for rating and reviewing the brand. Alternatively, they may be given more control over the features of the service they are buying. Anything that favourably affects the outcome and a customer's personal satisfaction provides a strong incentive for their continuing participation. Because loyalty to a brand depends on how appropriate and satisfying customers find their experience of the brand, it follows that the more loyal customers are, the more the brand should do for them. Being explicit about different loyalty levels helps manage expectations of each level and the reward structure also encourages customers to spend more in order to reach a higher level.

Glossary

Above the line (ATL) media	Advertising through mass media such as television, cinema, radio and print.
Assets	Anything owned by a company that has a financial value. Assets can be tangible, like buildings and machinery, or intangible, like a trademark, a brand name and intellectual property.
Average revenue per user (ARPU)	A measure used by mobile phone companies.
Balance sheet	A snapshot of a company's financial position on a given date. It shows the assets, liabilities and equity, and gives a picture of the financial health of the company.
Below the line (BTL) media	An incentive to purchase, expressed in cash or in kind, often of short duration. The focus is on direct means of communication, such as direct mail and e-mail.
Big data	Extremely large amounts of customer behaviour and sales data, often continuously collected, stored and analysed to predict future sales opportunities.
B2B (business-to-business)	Commercial transactions between businesses, such as a manufacturer and a wholesaler, or a wholesaler and a retailer.

B2C (business-to-consumer)	Businesses that sell products or services to consumers.
Business process outsourcing (BPO)	A way of subcontracting various business-related operations to a third party, often in a country with lower labour costs.
Capital expenditure (capex)	Expenditure relating to the improvement or acquisition of assets such as plant, machinery, or property.
Cash flow	A measure of the money flowing in and out of a business over a specific time period. It is one of the most important indicators of the health of a business.
Chief marketing officer (CMO)	A senior manager responsible for marketing activities in an organisation, generally reporting to the chief executive officer (CEO).
Cost of goods sold (COGS)	The direct costs of making a product or delivering a service.
Cost per thousand (CPM)	A measure used in analysing the effectiveness of media spend. The abbreviation CPM comes from cost per mille (in Latin mille means thousand).
Customer lifetime value (CLV)	The amount of revenue or profit that a company can expect a customer to generate over his or her lifetime.
Customer relationship management (CRM)	A model for managing a company's interactions with current and future customers.
Discounted cash flow (DCF)	A way of valuing a project, company, or asset using the concepts of the time value of money.

Discrete choice modelling (DCM)	A research and analysis method that tries to mimic real consumer decision-making processes by forcing respondents to trade off different product and price features. It is one of the most effective ways of assessing a consumer's willingness to pay for quality improvements in a product or service.
Executive brand council (EBC)	An organisational entity that is a forum for functional areas and business units to provide input and guidance on brand issues spanning those areas and business units.
EBIT	Earnings before interest and tax, with depreciation (loss of value on fixed assets, such as computers) and amortisation (loss of value of goodwill acquired in, for example, mergers and acquisitions) deducted.
EBITDA	Earnings before interest, taxes, depreciation and amortisation.
Economic value added (EVA)	A measure of economic profit above the opportunity cost of capital (if that money were used elsewhere, attracting an additional interest rate).
Employee value proposition (EVP)	A statement of the rewards and benefits that are received by employees in return for their performance in the workplace.
Equity	In finance, an ownership interest in an asset. Some business owners choose to sell equity in their business in order to raise money
Expenses	All costs associated with running the business not directly related to the cost of individual products or services

Fast-moving consumer goods (FMCG)	Everyday retail goods that are generally used up over a short period and therefore frequently purchased, including low-cost items such as groceries, soft drinks and toiletries. Sometimes called consumer packaged goods (CPG).
Gross profit	The value of sales minus cost of goods or services sold.
Gross revenues	The total amount of sales made per year.
Initial public offering (IPO)	The first sale of stock by a private company to the public, often issued by smaller, younger companies seeking the capital to expand. Also known as a public offering.
Key performance indicator (KPI)	Measures used by a company or industry to gauge or compare performance in terms of meeting its strategic and operational goals.
Like-on-like sales	A measure used by retailers to compare sales generated in one year with those generated the previous year. Also called year-on-year sales (Y-O-Y).
Net present value (NPV)	A useful measure of the potential for investment decisions for new segments or products. It is essentially a measurement of all future cash flow (revenues minus costs) that will be derived from a particular investment minus the cost of the capital investment. The actual cost of the capital investment is usually an agreed rate within each firm.
Net profit	Normally refers to the profit figure before deduction of corporation tax, in which case the term is often extended to net profit before tax or NPBT.

Net promoter score (NPS)	An advocacy measure used to assess the degree to which customers speak positively of a brand.
Revenue per available room (REVPAR)	A sales measure used in the hotel industry.
Return on investment (ROI)	A measure of the financial success of an investment or other activity. It is calculated as return divided by cost, and is often used to provide a basic overview of the success of marketing activities.
Selling, general and administrative expenses (SG&A)	The non-production costs of running a business (such as expenses).
Share of wallet	The proportion of money that customers spend on a particular brand compared with their overall spend within a specific product category.
Touch point	A point of contact or interaction between a business and its customers. Every touch point can positively or negatively reinforce or reduce customers' perception of the brand.
Turnover	Also known as revenue. The amount of money a company receives during a specific period; for example, a financial year.

Sources

1 Customer value management

Chief Marketing Officer executive survey, Senate, 2012

City.com, 2013

Dora, Sumit, Smit, Sven and Vigurie, Patrick, "Drawing a new road map for growth", *McKinsey Quarterly*, 2011

Tesco.com, Annual Report 2012

Webb, Alex, "Porsche Carmaking Profit Jumps 22% as Cayenne Sales Soar", Bloomberg, March 2012

2 Return on investment: measurement and analytics

IBM Institute for Business Value, "From stretched to strengthened", IBM Chief Marketing Officers survey, 2011

Leahy, Sir Terry, *Management in 10 Words*, Random House Business, 2012

Lloyds Banking Group, Outcome of Strategic Review", June 30th 2011

McAfee, Andrew and Brynjolfsson, Erik, "Big Data: The management revolution", *Harvard Business Review*, October 2012

McKinsey Global Institute, "Big data: the next frontier for innovation, competition and productivity", 2011

Nichols, Wes, "Advertising Analytics 2.0", *Harvard Business Review*, March 2013

Reichheld, Frederick F., "The One Number You Need to Grow", *Harvard Business Review*, December 2003

3 Barriers to growth

DeBeers.com, 2012

Kahneman, Daniel, *Thinking Fast and Slow*, Penguin, 2011

Lindstrom, Martin, *Buyology: How Everything We Believe About Why We Buy is Wrong*, Random House Business, 2009

Spreitzer, Gretchen and Porath, Christine, "Happy versus crappy", *Harvard Business Review*, March 2012

Telenav.com press release, "Survey Finds One-Third of Americans More Willing to Give Up Sex Than Their Mobile Phones", August 3rd 2011

www.brandkeys.com/archive/2012-customer-loyalty-winners

4 Targeting customers and external stakeholders

Costello, Sam, "Total number of iPods sold all-time", www.ipod.about.com, 2012

Duhigg, Charles, "How Companies Learn Your Secrets", *New York Times Magazine*, February 2012

The Economist, "Fashion forward. Zara, Spain's most successful brand, is trying to go global", The Economist.com, March 2012

Experian.com, 2012

Havas Media, "Meaningful brands index", havasmedia.com, 2011

IBM Institute for Business Value, op. cit.

The Wharton School, University of Pennsylvania, "Chipotle Mexican Grill", www.wiki.wharton.upenn.edu, 2013

5 Market opportunities for growth

ACG.org, "Mergers and acquisitions", August 2010

Google.com, investor relations, 2006

Redbull.com, 2013

Reuters.com, "L'Oréal aims to earn $1.3 bln in sales in India by 2020", January 2013

Reuters.com, "Nokia and Apple share financial performance", 2012

6 Proposition definition

Forbes.com, "10 Reasons Why Facebook Bought Instagram", November 2012

IBM.com, January 2013

Pearson Education, "Toothpaste Industry Market Report", Canada, 2007

Ries, Al and Trout, Jack, Positioning: The Battle for Your Mind, McGraw-Hill Professional, 2001

Stengel, Jim, Grow: How Ideals Power Growth and Profit at the World's Greatest Companies, Crown Business, 2011

7 Brand portfolio growth

DailyMail.com, "Cheap own labels overtake branded goods at the shops as consumers try to make their budgets go further", May 2012

Dawson, Thomas, "Private Label Brands: The future leaders of retail?", Brandstrategyinsider.com, May 2012

FashionUnited.co.uk, "Giorgio Armani shows no sign of slowing down", May 2012

Jaguar Land Rover, Annual Investor Presentation, www.jaguarlandrover.com, 2012

Tesco.com, 2013

Toyota.com, Annual Report 2012

Volkswagen.com, Annual Report 2006

Whatcar.com, UK, 2013

8 Growth through employee engagement

Bill Taylor, "Hire for attitude, train for skill", HBR Blog Network, www.blogs.hbr.org, February 2011

Cain, Susan, Quiet: The Power of Introverts in a World That Can't Stop Talking, Viking, 2012

CNN.com, "Carlos Ghosn: Nissan's turnaround artist", June 2005

Corporate Executive Board, "The Role of Employee Engagement in the Return to Growth", www.businessweek.com, August 2010

Corporate Leadership Council, "Attracting and retaining critical talent segments: Building a competitive employment value proposition", White Paper, 2006

Csíkszentmihályi, Mihály, Flow: The Psychology of Optimal Experience, Harper Perennial Modern Classics, 2008

Edman, Alex, "Does the stock market fully value intangibles? Employee satisfaction and equity prices", The Wharton School, University of Pennsylvania, 2011

Fortune India, June 2012

Furness, Ashley, interview with Diana Oreck of Ritz-Carlton, cxjourney.blogspot.co.uk, 2012

Gallup Survey, "What Really Drives Financial Success", www.businessjournal.gallup.com, 2012

Heskett, James L., Sasser, W. Earl Junior and Schlesinger, Leonard A., *The Service Profit Chain: How Leading Companies Link Profit and Growth to Loyalty, Satisfaction, and Value*, The Free Press, 1997

International Association of Business Communicators, Employee Engagement Survey, www.iabc.com, 2012

The Nissan way, Nissan-global.com, 2013

Peppers, Don and Rogers, Martha, *Managing Customer Relationships: A Strategic Framework*, Wiley, 2011

Smarter Workforce Conference Proceedings, Kenexa.com, 2012

Towers Watson, 2012 Global Workforce Study, www.towerswatson.com, 2013.

Zappos customer service analysis, customerservicescoreboard.com, 2013

9 Growth through customer engagement

12thinktank.com, "L2 digital m-commerce", 2013

Adams, Paul, "The real life social network: Taking social media from talk to action", *Harvard Business Review*, 2011

Bizreport.com, Mobile payments, 2013

Businessinsider.com, "how-people-use-smartphones", April 2013

Businesstoday.in "Entrenched in the digital world", February 2013

Cap Gemini, World Payments Report, 2012

CMO.com, "Fidelity Investments marketing leads with digital", September 2012

Coca-Cola company reports, www.businesswire.com, 2012

Coca-Cola liquid and linked video, www.youtube.com/watch?v=LerdMmWjU_E

Gartner Research, Mobile & Wireless, 2012

Guardian.com, "Study: less than 1% of the world's data is analysed, over 80% is unprotected", 2013

HBR Blog Network, "Ford recently wrapped the Fiesta", www.blogs.hbr.org, January 2010.

Imediaconnection.com "How American Express saw amazing returns by giving back", February 2012

ITU, ICT Facts and Figures, www.itu.int, 2013

MacMillan, Gordon, "Oreo scores big win on Super Bowl night with Twitter power-out ad", *Marketing Magazine*, February 2013

Mims, Christopher, "Google: Psy's 'Gangnam style' has earned $8 Million on YouTube alone", businessinsider.com, January 2013

Newmediatrendwatch.com, "World mobile phone usage: patterns and demographics", 2013

Nordstrom Annual Report, 2012

RetailSales report, www.retailsails.com, 2012

Spencer, Neil, "How much data is created every minute?", visualnews.com, 2012

Starbucks.com, Annual Report 2012

Techchrunch.com, "Mobile Milestone: The Number of Smartphones in Use Passed 1 Billion in Q3", 2012

www.youtube.com/watch?v=PKUDTPbDhnA

10 Growing service-based brands

Amazon.com, Annual Report, 2012

Avis.com, Annual Report, 2012

Business.mapsofindia.com, Service sector growth rate, February 2013

Cabincrew.com, Ryanair passenger figures, 2012

CNN.money.com, *Fortune* 500, company profits, 2012

Flightontime.info

Management.fortune.cnn.com, "Your table is waiting at OpenTable", March 2012

Mashable.com, "tasti-D-lite rewards", January 2010

Ryanair.com, Annual Report, 2012

UK Marketing Society, Giffgaff case study, 2012

Figures

Sources are given at the bottom of each figure except for those compiled by the author with any necessary permissions.

Further reading

Aaker, David, *Brand Portfolio Strategy: Creating Relevance, Differentiation, Energy, Leverage, and Clarity*, Free Press, 2004.

Baudrillard, J., *The Consumer Society: Myths and Structures*, Sage, 1991.

Bourdieu, Pierre, *Distinction: A Social Critique of the Judgement of Taste*, Routledge, 1984.

Cialdini, Robert, *Influence: The Psychology of Persuasion*, Collins Business, 2006.

Collins, Jim, *Good to Great*, Random House, 2001.

Csíkszentmihályi, Mihaly, *Flow: The Psychology of Optimal Experience*, Harper & Row, 1990.

Davenport, Thomas H. and Harris, Jeanne G., *Competing on Analytics*, Harvard Business School Press, 2007.

Doyle, Peter, *Value Based Marketing*, John Wiley & Sons, 2000.

Doyle, Peter, *Marketing Management and Strategy*, Prentice Hall, 2002.

Ellwood, Iain, *The Essential Brand Book*, Kogan Page, 2002.

Ellwood, Iain, "Brand Strategy", in *Brands and Branding*, Rita Clifton (ed.), Profile Books, 2009.

Ellwood, Iain and Shekar, Sheila, *Wonder Woman: Marketing Secrets for the Trillion Dollar Customer*, Macmillan, 2008.

Fisher-Buttinger, Claudia and Vallaster, Christine, *Connective Branding*, Wiley, 2008.

Furnham, Adrian, *All in the Mind: The Essence of Psychology*, Wiley, 1986.

Goleman, Daniel, "Leadership that gets results", *Harvard Business Review*, March 2000.

Heskett, James L., Sasser, W. Earl Junior, and Schlesinger, Leonard A., *The Service Profit Chain: How Leading Companies Link Profit and Growth to Loyalty, Satisfaction, and Value*, The Free Press, 1997.

Heskett, James L., Sasser, W. Earl and Wheeler, Joe, *The Ownership Quotient: Putting the Service Profit Chain to Work for Unbeatable Competitive Advantage*, Harvard Business School Press, 2008.

Hooley, Graham J., Saunders, John A. and Piercy, Nigel F., *Marketing Strategy and Competitive Positioning*, Prentice Hall, 1998.

Hoyer, Wayne D. and MacInnis, Deborah J., *Consumer Behaviour*, Houghton Mifflin, 2001.

Kapferer, J.N., *Strategic Brand Management: Creating and Sustaining Brand Equity Long Term*, Kogan Page, 1996.

Kotter, John, *Leading Change: The Essential Introduction to Organisational Change Management*, Harvard Business School Press, 1998.

Light, Lawrence Martin and Kiddon, Joan, *Six Rules for Brand Revitalisation*, Prentice Hall, 2009.

Lindstrom, Martin, *Buyology: How Everything We Believe About Why We Buy is Wrong*, Random House Business, 2009.

Maslow, Abraham H., *Motivation and Personality*, Longman, 1987.

McAfee, Andrew and Brynjolfsson, Erik, "Big Data: The management revolution", *Harvard Business Review*, October 2012.

McKinsey & Co, *Valuation: Measuring and Managing the Value of Companies*, 4th edition, Wiley, 2005.

McKinsey Global Institute, *Big data: the next frontier for innovation, competition and productivity*, McKinsey & Co, 2011.

McCluhan, Marshall, *The Medium is The Massage: An Inventory of Effects*, with Quentin Fiore, Bantam, 1967.

Milligan, Andy and Smith, Shaun, *Bold: How to be Brave in Business and Win*, Kogan Page, 2011.

Packard, V., *The Hidden Persuaders*, Penguin, 1991.

Pine, B. Joseph II and Gilmore, James H., *The Experience Economy*, Harvard Business Review Press, 2011.

Ries, Al and Trout, Jack, *The Battle for Your Mind*, McGraw-Hill Professional, 2001.

Reichheld, Frederick F., "The One Number You Need to Grow", *Harvard Business Review*, December 2003.

Rumelt, Richard, *Good Strategy, Bad Strategy*, Profile Books, 2011.

Index

A

above the line (ATL) media 150–151, 185

Accenture, brand proposition 99

acquisitions see mergers and acquisitions

Adidas, competitive differentiation 95

advertising
online 25
television 9, 21, 151, 153–154

advocacy analysis 33–34

airline industry
loyalty programmes 162–163
seat occupancy 179

Airmiles 163

Aldi, own-label brands 113

Alexa 36

Alico, sale to MetLife 104

Altria 130

Amazon
customer loyalty 162
one-click checkout (branded hallmark) 167, 180–181
sub-brands 117
Zappos 138, 142

American Express
brand portfolio management 119, 120–121, 183–184
customer engagement 11
social engagement 156–157

AOL, Bebo purchase and sale 82

Apple
brand loyalty 67, 95
brand portfolio management
naming convention 115
through own retail outlets 126
iPod introduction 53, 76
loss aversion 45
Nike co-branding 63
NPS scoring of stores 34
online store, one-click licence 180–181
retail stores 79–80, 126, 167, 170
smartphones 80–81

apps, use of 164

assets 185

AstraZeneca
brand proposition 103–104
employee engagement 147

AT&T, brand name 130

ATL (above the line) media 150–151, 185

attitudinal segmentation 57
attribution modelling 37
Audi
   brand portfolio management
      107, 120
   brand proposition 99
authenticity 96–97, 102
automation (of services) 180–181
average revenue per user (ARPU)
   185
Avis
   brand proposition 99
   maximising rental time 177
Aviva, sales channels 128

B
B2B (business-to-business) 185
   customer segmentation 60
   digital media marketing 171
B2C (business-to-consumer)
   186
baby-boomers 101
balance sheet 185
   intangible brand assets 29–32
Bang & Olufsen, brand extension
   127–128
Bank of America 115
banking industry, online account
   management 181
basket size 6
   see also cross-selling; upselling
BCG business matrix 18–20
Bebo 82
behaviour, employee see
   employee engagement
below the line (BTL) media
   150–151, 185
Bic 45–46

big data 12, 185
   real-time analytics 36–38
   use 24–25, 32–33
Blakely, Sarah 81
BMW
   brand portfolio management
      47, 107, 112, 115, 117
   credibility 96
   customer experience 165
   customer targeting 54
   Rolls-Royce acquisition 113
boardrooms, marketers' strategic
   role 1, 15, 51, 72
Bosch, brand extension 128
BPO (business process
   outsourcing) 11–12, 186
brand architecture 107, 114–116
brand divestment 130–131
brand extension 45–49, 75, 122–129
   see also product(s),
      development
Brand Finance 29–30, 31
brand identity 7, 115–116
brand loyalty 95
brand momentum (BM) 30
brand partnerships 63–64, 126
brand portfolio management
   assessment 116–121, 117
      decision-tree tool 118
      portfolio opportunity matrix
         119
   brand architecture 114–116
   strategies 106–114
brand proposition
   company authenticity 96–97,
      102
   competitive differentiation
      94–96

customer relevance 93–94
defining statements 98–102
extending 124
hallmarks 167, 168
higher purpose 96, 100–102, 104
message matrix 103
piloting 172–173
purpose and value 90–92, 102
sub-messages 102–103
brand valuation 29–32
BrandBeta index 29–30
brands
  anchoring 48–49
  budget brands 126–129
  categories 106–107
  consumer perceptions 152–153
  corporate 106–112
  DNA 97
  global versus local strategies
    71–75, 87–88
  own-label 7–8, 113–114, 128–129
  product (proposition) 112
  standalone 113
  sub-brands 112, 122
  switching 42–43
BrandZ (Millward Brown) 30,
  31
British Airways
  additional services 183
  brand proposition 96, 99, 126
BTL (below the line) media
  150–151, 185
budget brands 126–129
bundled offers 68
Burberry, social media
  engagement 156, 159
Burger King, competitive
  differentiation 94

business process outsourcing
  (BPO) 11–12, 186

C
Cain, Susan 142
campaign effectiveness analysis
  14
capital expenditure (capex) 86,
  186
Capital One 136
Carphone Warehouse,
  recruitment 135
Carrefour
  brand proposition 80
  language 116
cash flow 2, 186
Caterpillar 46–47
chief marketing officer (CMO)
  186
Chipotle 60–62
Citibank 10–11
Citroën, home market 74
cloud-based computing 155
CLV (customer lifetime value) 4–5,
  186
co-branding 63, 110, 126
Coca-Cola
  brand portfolio management
    106
  competitive differentiation 95
  social marketing 158
cognitive ease 41–42
communication, internal 146–147
company brand see corporate
  brands
competition, overcoming 98–99
compound annual growth rate
  (CAGR) 73

conjoint choice analysis *see*
discrete choice modelling
(DCM)
consumer packaged goods (CPG)
see fast-moving consumer
goods (FMCG)
consumers *see* customers
content creation and sharing 152,
155, 158
core markets 73
corporate brands 106–112
cost of goods sold (COGS) 186
cost per thousand (CPM) 186
Crest toothpaste, brand
proposition 93–94
CRM (customer relationship
management) 186
data systems 12–14
cross-selling 6, 7–8, 67
conditions for success 69–70
Csíkszentmihályi, Mihály 144, 145
customer experience 164–168
improvement process 168–173
customer lifetime value (CLV)
4–5, 186
customer mobility 43
customer relationship
management (CRM) 186
data systems 12–14
customer segmentation 48, 54
attitudinal analysis 57
benefits of targeting 51–53
business-to-business (B2B) 60
demographic analysis 54–56
golden rules 58–60
profiling and behavioural
analysis 13–14
usage analysis 56

see also targeting
customer value management
4–6
customers
acquiring 9–11
as brand advocates 11, 33–34, 95,
160–161
brand perceptions 91, 152
engagement 11, 150–151, 156–160
expectations 169, 177
online service delivery
180–183
service-based brands 179–181
fear of loss 43–44
influences on 153
involvement in product
development 76–77
peer-group reviews 10
profiling and behavioural
analysis 13–14
profitability 4–6, 12
relationships 8–9
research 21–22, 43, 93
satisfaction 10
segmentation *see* segmentation
in service profit chain 133
targeting 51–53
value and profitability analysis
48
cut through 94
CVS pharmacy chain, revenue
per square foot 170–171

D
data mining 24–25, 32–33
data protection 13
data systems 13, 17–18, 32–33,
38–39

DCM (discrete choice modelling)
23–24, 187
De Beers, brand anchoring 49
decision-making
boldness 45
brand anchoring 48–49
cognitive ease 41–42
customers 153
loss aversion 42–45
obstacles 40, 49–50
representativeness 46–48
Dell, data tracking 17–18, 25
demographic segmentation 54–56
departmental organisation 12
deprivation research 43
development costs 85–86
Diageo, brand portfolio
management 107
digital media 151–156
marketing investment budget
171
Direct Line
brand portfolio management
130–131
sales strategy 44
discounted cash flow (DCF) 186
discrete choice modelling (DCM)
23–24, 187
Disney World, customer
expectations 177
diversification 79–83
Dove
brand extension 75, 122–123
brand proposition 100
branded hallmark 167
DunnHumby 32
Dunstone, Charles 135
Dyson, brand proposition 96–97

E
e-newsletters 12
earned media 152–153
earnings before interest and tax
(EBIT) 187
easyJet 69, 128
eBay, seller/buyer evaluation
system 182
EBIT 187
EBITDA 187
EBITDA bridge 26
economic value added (EVA) 187
Edmans, Alex 132–133
emerging markets 9, 75
emotional appeal 8, 100
employee engagement
changing behaviour 139–140,
143
empowerment 143–146
guiding principles 138–140
leadership influence 141–143
measurement 147–148
programmes 133–135, 141, 142
in service profit chain 133
employee value proposition (EVP)
133, 137–138, 187
employees 61
capability and task difficulty
144
churn rate 147
communication 146–147
see also internal
communication
as emotional owners of the
business 144
induction training 133
motivation concerns 101
recruitment 135–137

training 133
turnover 144
see also employee engagement
equity 187
Ericsson 11–12
ethnographic research 93
Eurostar, customer expectations 180
EVP (employee value proposition) 133, 137–138, 187
executive brand council (EBC) 187
expenses 187
expert advocates 161–162

F
Facebook
  content creation and sharing 155
  customer engagement 37
fashion brands 74, 91, 126–127
fast-moving consumer goods (FMCG) 188
  big data use 25
  brand propositions 98
  product differentiation 78
  response to own-label brands 114
FedEx, brand damage 158–159
Ferrari 47
Fidelity, marketing budget 171, 172
First Direct, customer loyalty 162
first-mover (first to market) advantage 75–77, 81
flow (mental state) 144
fluency (decision-making) 41–42
Ford
  brand logos 116
  digital media budget 171

Forever 21 91
Foursquare 163
fragrance industry 47
Frei, Frances 181

G
General Electric (GE)
  NPS of customer service 34
  opportunity matrix 83
generation X 101
generation Y 101
Ghosn, Carlos 143
  see also Nissan
Giffgaff, member scheme 182–183
Gillette, platform-driven growth 78–79
Gilmore, James 8
Giorgio Armani, brand extension 126–127
global brands, marketing strategies 87–88
global reach 74
Godrej, marketing strategy 87–88
Goethe, Johann Wolfgang von 142
Google
  employee engagement 145–146
  product development 76–77
  YouTube purchase 81–82, 113
Google Analytics 36
government, as stakeholder 62
Gowar, Michael 164
Grey Goose vodka 43
gross profit 188
gross revenues 188
Grounsell, Dominic 159
growth markets
  analysis of 72–74, 88
  m-commerce 164

growth strategies
  market expansion 71–75
  market penetration 19–20, 30,
    67–70, 109
  product development 75–79,
    85–86, 123–124
  see also brand extension
  product diversification 79–83

H
Haier 62–63
hallmarks, branded 167, 168
halo effect 7
Harley Davidson 46–47
Harrah's, recruitment 137
Heskett, Jim 132
high-growth markets 73, 87
higher purpose brand
  propositions 96, 100–102, 104
Hilton Worldwide, brand
  portfolio management 108, 109
Hipstamatic 92
Hitwise 36
Holiday Inn
  brand extension 127
  Starbucks partnership 63
Home Depot, customer
  relationship management
  (CRM) 12, 157
home market 74
horizontal diversification 80
hotel industry
  customer expectations 179
  staff turnover 144
HSBC, brand proposition 99–100,
  107
Hsieh, Tony 142, 148
  see also Zappos

Hyundai
  branded hallmark 167
  marketing strategy 44

I
IBM, brand proposition 101–102,
  107
ICICI Bank, employee
  engagement 146
importance versus performance
  analysis 58
incremental improvements 45
ING Direct
  demerging of Voya 104
  growth strategy 72–73
  North American business
    model 136
initial public offering (IPO) 188
innovation strategy 78–79
insight gathering 16, 17–18
Instagram 92
insurance aggregator sites 14, 44,
  68
Interbrand 31
InterContinental Hotels Group
  (IHG)
  brand proposition 97, 99
  employees 135–136
  loyalty scheme 5
  sub-branding strategy 71–72
internal audiences 58
  see also boardrooms, marketers'
    strategic role
internal communication 146–147
internet usage 154, 181
investment costs 86
investment prioritisation analysis
  17, 18–20, 72–73

investors, as stakeholders 62

J
Jaguar 121–122, 129–130
jargon 41
Jobs, Steve 45

K
Kahneman, Daniel 42
Kelleher, Herb 135
key performance indicators (KPIs) 17, 188
Kochhar, Chanda 146
Kodak 81
Kuhlmann, Arkadi 136

L
Land Rover 121–122, 129–130
language 116
Lavazza, brand differentiation 128
leadership, influence on employee engagement 141–143
Lexus, brand management 47, 113, 125
life cycle, product 77–78, 78
Light, Larry 68, 135–136
like-on-like sales 188
Lindstrom, Martin 44
L.L. Bean, customer service 176
Lloyds Banking Group 26
logos 115–116
loss aversion 42–45
loyalty analysis 14
loyalty programmes 5, 9, 162–163
Tesco 32

M
m-commerce 164

market expansion 71–75
market penetration 19–20, 30, 67–70, 109
market positioning 91–92
market research 21–22
marketing
above the line (ATL) activities 150–151
below the line (BTL) activities 150–151
boardrooms perceptions 1, 15, 51, 72
campaign effectiveness analysis 14
commercial context 17, 21–26
digital media budget 171
investment strategy 88
media effectiveness analysis 34–36, 168–169
paid and earned media 151–153
Maslow, Abraham (motivation theory) 100
master brand strategy 108–112
mature markets 9–11, 19, 87
McDonald's
brand extension 69, 124
brand portfolio management 122
brand proposition 99
Chipotle investment 62
competitive differentiation 94
customer expectations 177, 179
price promotions 68
McKinsey opportunity matrix 83–84
media communications
above the line (ATL) media 150–151, 185

below the line (BTL) media
150–151, 185
budget 171
earned media 152–153
effectiveness analysis 34–36,
168–169
paid media 151–152
member gets member
programmes 10–11
Mercedes-Benz
brand portfolio management
108, 110–111
branded hallmark 167
mergers and acquisitions
brand management 113, 117,
129–130
message matrix 103–104
MetLife, purchase of Alico 104
Microsoft
brand extension 127
Mr Excel (expert advocate)
162
Millward Brown (BrandZ) 30, 31
mobile data 37
mobile marketing 163–164
mobile payments 164
mobile phones
customer profitability 6
market share 80–81
usage 154–155, 163–164
money-off vouchers 13
Mosaic classification system 55
Motorola 80
Movement for Self-esteem 100
Mr Porter, customer targeting
53–54
Musk, Elon 82

N
names, product 115–116, 119–120
near-field communications 37
Nectar card 163
Net-a-Porter 53–54
net present value (NPV) 5, 188
net profit 188
net promoter score (NPS) 33–34,
41–42, 189
Nike
Apple co-branding 63
competitive differentiation 95
Nintendo Wii 115
Nissan
brand extension 125
employee engagement 133–135
Nokia 19, 80–81, 100
non-price-driven offers 177–178
Nordstrom, customer service
hallmark 167
Norton anti-virus software,
customer ratings 161–162
NPS (net promoter score) 33–34,
41–42, 189
NPV (net present value) 5, 188

O
O$_2$
customer relationship
management (CRM) 13
employee engagement 140
Ocado 13
online service delivery 180–183
operating costs 86
operating profit growth 3–4
opportunity assessment 83–88
optimal experience flow diagram
145

Oreo, customer engagement
153–154
organisational culture 138
outsourcing 11–12
own-label brands 7–8, 113–114,
128–129

P
paid media 151–152
Pan Am 97
partnerships 62–64
Peppers, Don 136
Pepsi Cola, competitive
differentiation 95
perfume industry 47
person to person sharing 155–156
Pfizer 107
Philip Morris 130
Philips, master-brand strategy 110
Pierre Cardin, brand extension
127
piloting 172–173
Pine, B. Joseph 8
Pinterest 38, 157
plain (business) English 41–42
platform-driven growth 78–79
Porsche 8–9, 114
Porsche, Ferdinand Alexander 126
portable music players 76
portfolio analysis 18–20, 72–73
positioning, market 91–92
potential value assessment 83–88
premium brands 124–126
pressure groups 65
price-comparison websites 14,
44, 68
price elasticity 24
price sensitivity modelling 79

pricing strategies
promotional 68
three-tier brands 128–129
prioritisation analysis 17, 18–20,
72–73
Procter & Gamble
brand portfolio management
107, 108, 109
cross-selling 70
NPS of brands 34
product development 78
product uses 69
social media use 37
see also Crest toothpaste,
brand proposition; Gillette,
platform-driven growth
product choice see discrete choice
modelling (DCM)
product(s)
awareness of 10
brands 112
development 75–79, 85–86,
123–124
see also brand extension
diversification 79–83
life cycles 77–78
markets 74
naming 115–116, 119–120
rating systems 160–161
uses 69
profitability
and customer loyalty 132
and employee engagement 132
profitability analysis 14
profits, growth 3–4
Progressive Casualty Insurance
Company 176–177
promotional pricing 68

proposition brands 112
PruHealth 182
Psy, YouTube dance video 154
purchase decisions, influences
   on 153
purchase frequency 6
purchase funnel analysis 24,
   27–28

Q
qualitative research 93

R
Ralph Lauren 47, 127
Range Rover 121–122
rating systems 160–161
reach curve 35
real-time data analytics 36–38
recruitment 135–137
Red Bull 71
regression analysis 22–23
regulators 65
Reichfield, Fred 33
Renault partnership with Toyota 63
representativeness 46–48
reputation management 65
retail industry 8, 32, 52–53, 80, 113,
   114, 129, 193
   m-commerce 164
   online shopping 181
Return on investment (ROI) 189
revenue growth 3–4
   predicting 84–85
revenue per available room
   (REVPAR) 189
revenue per employee 147
Ries, Al 92
risk aversion of marketers 44–45

risks
   affect on cash flow 2–3
   master brand strategy 112
Ritz-Carlton
   brand proposition 100
   employee engagement 143–144
Royal Bank of Scotland, Direct
   Line divestment 130–131
rules of thumb 46–48
Ryanair 178, 179

S
Sainsbury's
   employee engagement 143
   own-label brands 113
sales analysis 13
Samsung 80, 116
Sasser, Earl 132
SatMetrix 33
scenario planning 25–26, 104
Schlesinger, Leonard 132
search engine linked advertising
   151–152
segmentation 48, 54
   attitudinal analysis 57
   benefits of targeting 51–53
   business-to-business (B2B) 60
   demographic analysis 54–56
   golden rules 58–60
   profiling and behavioural
      analysis 13–14
   stakeholders 60–63, 65
   usage analysis 56
   see also targeting
self-service 181
selling, general and
   administrative expenses
   (SG&A) 189

service-based brands
  brand proposition 96, 98, 101
  customer expectations 179–181
  employees 178
  marketing function role 177
  online delivery 180–183
  price management 178
  processes 175–178
  product/service levels 183
service profit chain 133
share of wallet 7, 9–11, 189
shareholder value creation 2
Siemens, co-branding 126
simplicity 14–15, 90
Singapore Airlines, customer
  experience 165
Small Business Saturday 156–157
smartphones *see* mobile phones
Smith, Fred (FedEx founder) 96
social marketing 157–162
social media 10, 12–13, 37
  consumer recommendations
    and opinions 152–153, 160–161
  customer conversations 102–103
  special interest groups 65
social-media marketing 157–159
social responsibility 96, 100–102,
  104
Sony, retail outlets 126
Sony Walkman 76
Spanx 81
special interest groups 65
Spicejet 92
sponsorship events 10, 71
Sprint 11–12
stakeholders
  brand proposition and
    supporting messages 102–104

segmentation 60–63, 65
standalone brands 113
Starbucks
  customer experience 165–166
  at Holiday Inn 63
  service personalisation 180
Stengel, Jim 100
Still, David (Vodafone) 98, 160
strategic choice analysis *see*
  discrete choice modelling
  (DCM)
strategic marketing analytics 17
sub-brands 112, 122
Subway, loyalty programme 163
supermarkets 7–8, 13, 32, 80
suppliers 62
Symantec, customer ratings
  161–162

T
tablet usage *see* mobile phones
Target (US store)
  cross-selling 7–8
  customer segmentation 59
  own-label brands 114
targeting
  benefits 51–53
  see also segmentation
Tasti D-lite, loyalty scheme 163
Tata, brand portfolio management
  121–122, 129–130
Telenav 43
television advertising 9, 21, 151,
  153–154
Tesco
  balanced scorecard data
    tracking 17
  Clubcard loyalty scheme 32

DunnHumby data-mining
agency 32
financial services 8
Florence & Fred clothing range
8
own-label brands 113–114, 128
Tesla Motors, category
transformation 82
The Ivy, Beverley Hills 8
touch point 189
touch point analysis 23–24, 169,
170
Towers Watson Global Workforce
Study (2012) 132, 148
Toyota
brand range 73
credibility 96
Lexus brand 47, 113, 125
Renault partnership 63
transformations, product category
80–83
travel industry 7, 96, 97, 99, 127,
169
TripAdvisor 152, 161
Trout, Jack 92
trust 96–97
turnover 189
Tversky, Amos 42
Twitter
customer engagement 37
instantaneous nature 154, 155
Tasti D-lite loyalty scheme
163

U
Unilever
brand portfolio management
107

Dove
brand extension 75, 122–123
brand proposition 100
branded hallmark 167
upselling 6, 7, 8
conditions for success 70
see also cross-selling
usage segmentation 56

V
value brands 126–129
values *see* organisational culture
vertical integration 79–80
Virgin Atlantic
customer experience 8
market positioning 91–92, 96
vertical integration 80
Visa, mobile payments 164
Vodafone
brand proposition 100
home market 74
local branding 87
partnership branding 64
Volkswagen
brand extension 125
customer service 176
Volkswagen Audi Group (VAG) 79
Volvo
brand name 130
brand proposition 102, 124

W
Walmart, own-label brands 129
washing powders
brand propositions 93
category transformation 82
product differentiation 78
website analytics 36–37

white labelling 80
Wii 115

Y
yield management 178
YouTube
   advertising revenues 154
   first-mover advantage 81
   Google acquisition 113

Z
Zappos 138, 142
Zara, customer targeting 52–53
Zingerman 41
zone, employees in the 144

"This book advances the vision of marketing management. In recognising the links between a business's operations and its customers, it demonstrates modern-day multi-functional management. It belongs on the bookshelves of all marketers and anyone who works with them." James L. Heskett, UPS Foundation Professor Emeritus, Harvard Business School

"Ellwood dentifies the brand and marketing fundamentals that help drive business growth." Larry Light, Chief Brands Officer, IHG, and former Global Chief Marketing Officer at McDonald's

"This important book clearly and effectively demonstrates that innovative brand marketing can lead the boardroom growth agenda and drive shareholder returns." Simon Smith, Regional Head of Corporate Communications (Asia), MetLife

"Provides valuable insights and practical techniques to help business leaders grow the top and bottom line." David Aaker, Vice-Chairman, Prophet, and author of Brand Relevance

"This book helps business leaders understand the value of marketing in achieving profitable growth. It shows how marketers' in-depth knowledge of customers gives them the key to unlock profits through building strong brands, ensuring employees' engagement and taking advantage of market opportunities." Simona Botti, Associate Professor of Marketing, London Business School

"What can be more relevant for today's executives than how to drive business growth through marketing? This book shows why and how marketing should have a seat at every boardroom table." Gabor Dani, Leader, Customer Centricity, Zurich Insurance

"Reveals the essential marketing truths that will help business executives increase shareholder value." David Still, Head of Brand Strategy, Vodafone

"A much needed and comprehensive guide to transforming business that puts marketing firmly at the centre stage of growth." Markus Kramer, Global Marketing Director, Aston Martin

"*Truly valuable ... provides a powerful framework to help business leaders grow the top and bottom line.*" Rita Clifton, Chairman, Populus, and former Chairman of Interbrand

"*Shows how and why brand marketing can lead to measurable business success.*" Paul Groves, Group Chief Marketing Officer, AIA

"*Marked by pioneering thinking and clear writing, this is a perceptive book by someone who has helped shape the marketing world.*" Adrian Furnham, Professor of Psychology, University College London

"*A category defining guide that is a must have for brand marketers and business leaders.*" John Allert, Group Brand Director, McLaren Formula 1 team

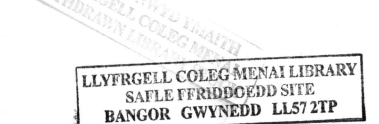